D0852079

IT HAPPENED TO ME

Series Editor: Arlene Hirschfelder

Books in the It Happened to Me series are designed for inquisitive teens digging for answers about certain illnesses, social issues, or lifestyle interests. Whether you are deep into your teen years or just entering them, these books are gold mines of up-to-date information, riveting teen views, and great visuals to help you figure out stuff. Besides special boxes highlighting singular facts, each book is enhanced with the latest reading lists, websites, and an index. Perfect for browsing, there are loads of expert information by acclaimed writers to help parents, guardians, and librarians understand teen illness, tough situations, and lifestyle choices.

1. *Epilepsy: The Ultimate Teen Guide,* by Kathlyn Gay and Sean McGarrahan, 2002.
2. *Stress Relief: The Ultimate Teen Guide,* by Mark Powell, 2002.
3. *Learning Disabilities: The Ultimate Teen Guide,* by Penny Hutchins Paquette and Cheryl Gerson Tuttle, 2003.
4. *Making Sexual Decisions: The Ultimate Teen Guide,* by L. Kris Gowen, 2003.
5. *Asthma: The Ultimate Teen Guide,* by Penny Hutchins Paquette, 2003.
6. *Cultural Diversity—Conflicts and Challenges: The Ultimate Teen Guide,* by Kathlyn Gay, 2003.
7. *Diabetes: The Ultimate Teen Guide,* by Katherine J. Moran, 2004.
8. *When Will I Stop Hurting? Teens, Loss, and Grief: The Ultimate Teen Guide to Dealing with Grief,* by Ed Myers, 2004.
9. *Volunteering: The Ultimate Teen Guide,* by Kathlyn Gay, 2004.
10. *Organ Transplants—A Survival Guide for the Entire Family: The Ultimate Teen Guide,* by Tina P. Schwartz, 2005.

11. *Medications: The Ultimate Teen Guide,* by Cheryl Gerson Tuttle, 2005.

12. *Image and Identity—Becoming the Person You Are: The Ultimate Teen Guide,* by L. Kris Gowen and Molly C. McKenna, 2005.

13. *Apprenticeship: The Ultimate Teen Guide,* by Penny Hutchins Paquette, 2005.

14. *Cystic Fibrosis: The Ultimate Teen Guide,* by Melanie Ann Apel, 2006.

15. *Religion and Spirituality in America: The Ultimate Teen Guide,* by Kathlyn Gay, 2006.

16. *Gender Identity: The Ultimate Teen Guide,* by Cynthia L. Winfield, 2007.

17. *Physical Disabilities: The Ultimate Teen Guide,* by Denise Thornton, 2007.

18. *Money—Getting It, Using It, and Avoiding the Traps: The Ultimate Teen Guide,* by Robin F. Brancato, 2007.

19. *Self-Advocacy: The Ultimate Teen Guide,* by Cheryl Gerson Tuttle and JoAnn Augeri Silva, 2007.

20. *Adopted: The Ultimate Teen Guide,* by Suzanne Buckingham Slade, 2007.

21. *The Military and Teens: The Ultimate Teen Guide,* by Kathlyn Gay, 2008.

22. *Animals and Teens: The Ultimate Teen Guide,* by Gail Green, 2009.

23. *Reaching Your Goals: The Ultimate Teen Guide,* by Anne Courtright, 2009.

24. *Juvenile Arthritis: The Ultimate Teen Guide,* by Kelly Rouba, 2009.

25. *Obsessive-Compulsive Disorder: The Ultimate Teen Guide,* by Natalie Rompella, 2009.

26. *Body Image and Appearance: The Ultimate Teen Guide,* by Kathlyn Gay, 2009.

27. *Writing and Publishing: The Ultimate Teen Guide,* by Tina P. Schwartz, 2010.

28. *Food Choices: The Ultimate Teen Guide,* by Robin F. Brancato, 2010.

29. *Immigration: The Ultimate Teen Guide,* by Tatyana Kleyn, 2011.

30. *Living with Cancer: The Ultimate Teen Guide,* by Denise Thornton, 2011.

31. *Living Green: The Ultimate Teen Guide,* by Kathlyn Gay, 2012.

32. *Social Networking: The Ultimate Teen Guide,* by Jenna Obee, 2012.

SOCIAL NETWORKING

THE ULTIMATE TEEN GUIDE

JENNA OBEE

IT HAPPENED TO ME, NO. 32

THE SCARECROW PRESS, INC.
Lanham • Toronto • Plymouth, UK
2012

For Bow.

Published by Scarecrow Press, Inc.
A wholly owned subsidary of The Rowman & Littlefield Publishing Group, Inc.
4501 Forbes Boulevard, Suite 200, Lanham, Maryland 20706
www.rowman.com

10 Thornbury Road, Plymouth PL6 7PP, United Kingdom

British Library Cataloguing in Publication Information Available

Library of Congress Cataloging-in-Publication Data

Obee, Jenna, 1974–
  Social networking : the ultimate teen guide / Jenna Obee.
     p. cm. — (It happened to me ; no. 32)
  Includes bibliographical references and index.
  ISBN 978-0-8108-8120-4 (hbk. : alk. paper) — ISBN 978-0-8108-8121-1 (ebook)
  1. Internet and teenagers. 2. Online social networks. I. Title.
  HQ799.2.I5O24 2012
  004.67'80835—dc23   2011049875

∞™ The paper used in this publication meets the minimum requirements of American National Standard for Information Sciences—Permanence of Paper for Printed Library Materials, ANSI/NISO Z39.48-1992.

Printed in the United States of America

Contents

1   This Ain't Your Parents' Internet   7

2   Stay Safe and Be Smart   23

3   Stick Up for Yourself: Cyberbullying   55

4   If You're Friendly and You Know It: Keeping Up with Friends   77

5   Other Ways to Socialize with Friends Online   103

6   The Mobile World   119

7   How to Save the World   135

8   Homemade Movies: Manage Your Videos   147

9   Attune to the Tunes: Managing Your Music   165

10   Say Cheese! Manage Your Photos   177

11   Love Them, May as Well Follow Them: Celebrities   191

12   Get Those A's: Doing School   201

13   Have Fun, Play Games, Avoid Boredom   213

14   Kicking the Habit: When and How to Quit   229

15   The Internet: The Final Frontier?   241

Suggested Reading List   247

Index   249

About the Author   259

THIS AIN'T YOUR PARENTS' INTERNET

···

"It's to the point where you can have millions of friends
and never leave your house." —Bow, age 20

What Is "Social Media"?

A social media site is any website that allows you to comment, share, like, friend, or otherwise interact with the other members of the site. Social media sites are the ones that let you socialize online with friends or strangers. The

Social media sites let you socialize with your friends online.

Web 2.0

Web consultant Darcy DiNucci created the term *Web 2.0* in a 1999 article on the future of web design. She wrote, "The Web we know now, which loads into a browser window in essentially static screenfuls, is only an embryo of the Web to come. The first glimmerings of Web 2.0 are beginning to appear, and we are just starting to see how that embryo might develop. . . . The Web will also appear, in different guises, on your TV set . . . , your car dashboard . . . , your cell phone . . . , hand-held game machines . . . , and maybe even your microwave."[1]

most obvious example is Facebook, but social media also includes websites such as YouTube, Flickr, Twitter, wikis, chat rooms, game sites, your school website, ringtone websites, blogs, and much more. Any time that you are interacting with people on a website, doing more than just reading what's on the screen, you are using a social media site.

Social media is also called *Web 2.0* or *social networking*. The idea is that a website that allows you to participate and create your own content is a step beyond websites that you can only view. If the site is primarily about networking with other people, it's usually called a "social network."

Social networks include the things that teens do online—share about life, play games, chat with friends, listen to music, watch videos, and more—making such places a good place to find entertainment and hang out virtually. Studies show that youth ages 8 to 18 spend an average of 7.5 hours per day interacting with some kind of electronic device—and those studies didn't even take texting into consideration. "For most children, the daily log of media immersion would surpass time spent sleeping."[2]

As of June 2010, teens spend 80 percent of their Internet time on social networks. Of roughly 2 hours and 20 minutes a day on the Internet, 1 hour and 50 minutes goes to social networks.[3]

Statistics about Social Media

• 73 percent of online American teens aged 12 to 17 used an online social network website, a statistic that has continued to climb upward, from 55 percent in November 2006 and 65 percent in February 2008.[4]

According to the Facebook statistics count, in 2011

• 23,000,000,000 minutes were spent on Facebook each day;

• 1,000,000,000 items of content (web links, news stories, blog posts, notes, photos, etc.) were shared on Facebook each day;

• there were 130 friends per user (on average) on Facebook;

• if Facebook were a country, it would be third in the world by population; and

• 35 percent of Americans have a Facebook account.[5]

How Social Networking Is (Supposedly) Ruining Teenagers and the Future

As with any cultural change between generations, people are arguing whether social media is a good thing. Some feel that sitting in front of a computer to socialize is deteriorating teens' social skills and ability to communicate. Additionally, there are concerns that teens do not protect their privacy while online, and this is perceived as a serious problem for the future of the generation.

This issue is really about any use of the Internet as well as how culture changes. These are the activities that teens are doing more than adults; therefore, the alarm is in how teens are growing up differently from their parents. The major difference is that teens use the Internet and their electronic devices as tools to live their lives, using them to do things that their parents wouldn't think of. Most adults did not grow up

What Teens Are Saying

"I don't know if it's a good thing for our society. I mean this is, as far as I can see, where our society is heading and how you reach a mass majority of people. There's so much emphasis on the online. It seems like everything is there, and sometimes it is really convenient, but I think it might be ruining society too."
—Ariel, age 18

"I think my generation's dependence on the Internet is pathetic."
—Ava, age 16

using tools such as the Internet in that way and are therefore not as comfortable with the technology and have not integrated it as completely into their lives.

Social Skills

There are quite a few studies analyzing how teens use social media and how this is changing Western society. Overall, these studies are showing that social media is just another way of communicating and that teens are using it just as they communicate in their real-life interactions. Today's teens have grown up

What Adults Are Saying

"Far from hampering adolescents' social skills or putting them in harm's way, as many parents have feared, electronics appear to be the path by which children today develop emotional bonds, their own identities, and an ability to communicate and work with others. In fact, children most likely to spend lots of time on social media sites are . . . the healthiest psychologically, suggests an early, but accumulating, body of research."[6]
—Melissa Healy, *Los Angeles Times*

with daily Internet access and are therefore much more comfortable with the technology than previous generations are.

In May 2010, myYearbook.com users were polled about their habits both online and offline. The teens most dedicated to social

> **What Teens Are Saying**
>
> "The good thing is that you get more outgoing and I think Facebook kind of builds your social side."
> —Priyanka, age 15

networking, called *influencers*, made up about 15 percent of the respondents. The study found that influencers were 40 percent more likely than the average teen to attend a party and were 20 percent more likely to have had a friend visit their home in the previous week. Influencers were also more likely than the average teen to read, play games, or listen to music. "The survey dispels the notion that the most engaged teens on a social network are most likely to be home alone on a Saturday night; those teens who are most social online are most social offline," said Geoff Cook, CEO of myYearbook.[7]

"The majority of youth use new media to 'hang out' and extend existing friendships,"[8] says another study. The report urges parents to assist their children in using the tools of digital and social media, rather than attempt to block access to them, and it finds that the online world isn't nearly as frightening as parents may assume.

A task force of major players from many social networks as well as nonprofit organizations and universities wrote a report on the online safety of children in 2008. It found that "the Internet is a positive and powerful space for socializing, learning, and engaging in public life."[9] Additionally, minors who are most at risk online are the ones who are at risk in other parts of their lives as well.

The Internet can also give you the social interaction you need in a more comfortable setting. Friendships you maintain online can be very powerful. It is easier to say the hard things to people you can't see, so your online friends can get to you know you considerably better than your real-life friends. You also can overcome physical issues such as appearance to make friends as you have never

What Teens Are Saying

"I think that the abbreviations are an evolving stage in our society. It is not ruining teens writing skills, it is creating a new portion of the social language. It is where language meets the demands of an evolving fast-paced society looking for quick solutions." —Adam, age 17

"I don't want to know what you are doing every second of the day. I hate how every one of my friends or every teen is expected to have one, and if you don't, people act as if something is wrong with you. I like face-to-face communication, or at least voice-to-voice. I also think sites like Twitter and Facebook are ruining relationships and grammar." —Ariel, age 18

"I think that it's nonsense to say that netspeak is ruining teens' writing skills. Most teens can easily distinguish this is a text message, this is an English paper. On the other hand I was editing a school project submitted by my fellow Junior and they had spelled school 'skool,' so I may be completely wrong."
—Averill, age 18

"Usually I try to use pretty good grammar [online] so that I don't get into the habit of slacking off in school or anything else I write." —Bow, age 20

been able to before. Someone exceedingly shy in real life can be gregarious and popular online. That kid who barely speaks in school may be the huge fan fiction, or *fanfic*, writer you idolize on your favorite website!

The bottom line is that teens who are responsible and well behaved at home will be the same online and those bullying in school will likely bully online as well; it's your psychological makeup that determines how you behave both online and offline. Social networks have existed as long as humans have hung out in groups—the difference now is that our social networks use technology to be bigger and more inclusive than ever before.

"I remember and know people who put u in for you in school assignments. It is definitely destroying teens' vocab." —Daniel, age 17

"I do believe that netspeak and text language is ruining teens' spelling, grammar and punctuation. The majority of youth have no appreciation for the correct structure of sentences or spelling anymore when it's more convenient to abbreviate everything. Relying on spellcheck for school assignments seems all well and good, but most tests (especially the major ones) are still handwritten, and after seeing the nearly illegible essays, riddled with spelling errors, that some of my friends have submitted—I was actually shocked. Even the most basic skills are dying out with the increasing use of online communication."
—Grace, age 16

"English teachers have it so burned in to my brain that, if anything, my regular English slips into chatting with friends." —Jack C., age 14

"I think texting is really convenient, but I'd rather talk to someone in person than read what they've sent. Besides, those communication skills are crucial for the 'real world,' and our generation is losing that skill!" —Niki, age 15

Communication

Netspeak is the term used to identify simplified communication using electronic devices, including that on the Internet and in texting. It started with shortening common words or phrases in e-mail and chat rooms and has become commonly used in verbal conversations. Have you ever said "O-M-G" out loud? That's using netspeak in real life. This came about because the way that we talk in online interactions tends to mirror actual speech patterns rather than more formalized forms of communication, such as letters or school papers. For instance, you don't

Two Sides

"The world is changing every day in many different ways. Language is just one part of that change. My generation of txt writers are the future leaders, so if we decide to communicate in a way that is faster, more efficient and better for us, the older generation should not so quickly dismiss or ridicule the new language." —Carlos, age 16, in *The Record*[10]

"As the language evolves, necessary elements are being carelessly tossed away even though they are needed." —Nicole, age 16, in *The Record*[11]

use complete sentences when you speak aloud, so why would you in your textual conversations? It makes sense that terms you use in instant messaging would make their way into your verbal communication too.

Naomi Baron, a researcher at American University, did a study evaluating speech patterns in instant messaging conversations of college-age students. She found that 22 percent of messages were a single word and that many complete thoughts were broken up into multiple messages, giving a little bit of information in each part. Baron theorized that this method of conversation keeps the other person interested. She also found that it is common to have multiple topics going at the same time in a single conversation with a single person and that students can maintain multiple private conversations at once, all the while doing other tasks.

The argument that netspeak is making teenagers into bad writers comes from the idea that teens don't know when to use netspeak versus formal language. Some teens agree, including Annie, who said, "I think [netspeak] probably is affecting writing skills because good English just doesn't seem important or necessary any more." However, as Ava suggested, "the abbreviations are needed, because there are only a certain amount of characters allowed per text. I have not seen my spelling affected by texting, nor anyone I talk to. Most kids know when formal writing is

Is It Reading?[12]

- 25 percent of kids aged 9 to 17 think that texting back and forth with friends counts as reading, while only 8 percent of parents agree.
- 28 percent of those kids think that looking through postings or comments on social networking sites such as Facebook counts as reading; only 15 percent of parents agree.

required." You use a different tone and vocabulary when you're talking to your parents versus your friends, and writing for school is very different from writing for personal use. Just as you have learned what is acceptable at the dinner table, you need to learn what is acceptable in a formal essay. If in doubt, be more formal.

Reading online will only improve your ability to comprehend English and teach you new words. If you were to find books on each and every topic you investigate online, you would likely learn many of the same words. Writing online, whether in quick communication with friends or in comments or blogs, gives you practice writing and a keen sense of talking to your reader. Considering the audience while writing is a skill that your generation has always done and your teachers' had to consciously learn.

Texting can help you do better in school, too. Studies are finding that texters have better understanding of word reading, have a higher vocabulary, and are better at spelling because the phonetic nature of textspeak takes a higher awareness of the alphabet to encode. Researcher Sali Tagliamonte of the University of Toronto said, "Everybody thinks kids are ruining their language by using instant messaging, but these teens' messaging shows them expressing themselves flexibly through all registers. They actually show an extremely lucid command of the language. We shouldn't worry."[13]

Netspeak and multitasking while using the computer are teaching teens skills that will likely be useful in the future. Mizuko Ito, lead researcher on a MacArthur

> ## What Adults Are Saying
>
> "As educators move traditional written responses to literature into online forums, they find that students still use the literary discourse from the classroom, along with asserting their own personalities in their posts. Because students recognize that there is a social context for their work online, they often conform to certain roles or expectations without teacher prompting, because they want to impress their peers."[14]
> —Sheelah M. Sweeney in the *Journal of Adolescent and Adult Literacy*

Foundation study entitled "Living and Learning with New Media," told the *New York Times*, "It may look as though kids are wasting a lot of time hanging out with new media, whether it's on MySpace or sending instant messages, but their participation is giving them the technological skills and literacy they need to succeed in the contemporary world. They're learning how to get along with others, how to manage a public identity."[15]

Finally, there is the important point that languages change over time. You only need to read Shakespeare to know that people of today do not talk like they did 400 years ago. Vocabulary is changing even faster due to an increase in the speed of technological change; cell phones didn't exist 50 years ago, so there was no need to have a name for them. It is only the words that spread through the population that stick. In the future, when you have children and grandchildren you can barely understand, you can know that you were part of the generation to introduce and spread words such as *LOL* and *OMG*.

Privacy

"Media reports teem with stories of young people posting salacious photos online, writing about alcohol-fueled misdeeds on social networking sites, and publicizing other ill-considered escapades that may haunt them in the future.

What Teens Are Saying

"To be honest, I hate netspeak. When people talk like 'hey u, i wna c u 2mro @ 7 at AHS' it just seems to make them seem unintelligent. For me, it takes like twice as much time to use and understand the shorthand, so I don't see the point in using it. I'd rather just type out the intelligible, intelligent sounding sentences." —Annie, age 16

"I like emoticons, but netspeak gets on my nerve. I don't think it's that much harder to write out 'you,' and haha is an excellent way to indicate laughter, and you can also easily indicate degrees of laughter, for example hahahahahaha."
—Averill, age 18

"I use emoticons a lot, but I don't usually have altered grammar for online, it really annoys me WeN PPl TAlk LyK DI$ ON DA Pc because that's just ridiculous." —Grace, age 16

"I figure I might as well spell out the words, being a grammar nerd myself, so I'm usually pretty good about not transferring those acronyms into school assignments. Netspeak can surely be faster but I find it unnecessary, especially the really long acronyms." —Niki, age 15

These anecdotes are interpreted as representing a generation-wide shift in attitude toward information privacy."[16] Therefore, as Ariel Maislos, chief executive of a company offering an advertising-based phone service, told the *New York Times*, the assumption is that "young people . . . are less concerned with maintaining privacy than older people are."[17] It is up to each and every teen to prove them wrong, and you are already doing so.

A 2009 Pew Internet study showed that privacy is not as much a problem as assumed. A senior research specialist at Pew, Mary Madden, said, "Contrary to the popular perception that younger users embrace a laissez-faire attitude about

What Teens Are Saying

"I actually met my best friend over MySpace. (I know I should always be cautious when talking to strangers, but this was perfectly safe and one of the best things I've ever done.)" —Grace, age 16

"There are many teens . . . putting up provocative pictures of themselves on their social networking sites and then not putting any privacy settings on their home pages so that anyone can see them. I pay attention to privacy settings because I do care about who looks at my personal info." —Bow, age 20

their online reputations, young adults are often more vigilant than older adults when it comes to managing their online identities."[18] Another study found that 78 percent of teens feel in control of their privacy on social networking sites and 84 percent of parents feel that their teen is responsible about being private.

Another survey, this one of nearly 1,400 ten- to seventeen-year-olds, suggested that teens are sharing too much online, but then it explained that they usually share their first name, age, or e-mail address. Only 10 percent have given out more dangerous information, such as photos, school information, their phone number, or their last name. In a *Cnet* article on the study, Larry Magid said, "Considering that Facebook . . . actually requires use of real names and encourages posting photos and such information as school name, I don't find this at all shocking."[19]

Friendships

Before social media use, people were friends only with people whom they knew directly. Friendships formed via letters were uncommon and hard to maintain. The Internet has made it possible, even easy, to become friends with strangers who live on the other side of the world. This is a drastic change in how relationships work, and older generations don't necessarily understand that to you, an online friend is equal to a real-life friend.

> **Interesting Factoid**
>
> - 5,830 words in Facebook's privacy policy
> - 4,543 words in the US Constitution

When social media sites were brand new, back in the Friendster days, people friended anyone they could find no matter who she or he was. It was a numbers game, where people with friend counts higher than yours were considered more popular. It didn't take long for people to realize that this method was empty and unfulfilling. These days, people friend their friends. Maybe they meet someone new online and friend them too, but the connection is usually there before the friending happens.

Friendship is not based on where you interact, be it real life or online; it is based on the relationship you make with another person you have come to know well enough to call *friend*. Additionally, you don't maintain each friendship at the same level. You have your closest friends, those you communicate with regularly and probably know both online and offline. You also have friends with whom you keep in contact through a social media site because if you didn't, you wouldn't even be friends anymore. All of this is no different than it was 50 years ago, except that now technology allows for quicker and easier communication across distances, even if that distance is the next room.

Technological Skills

Consider that using social media sites and the Internet gives you experience and comfort using the tools of the future. Even if you don't go on to work for a computer company, computers will be a part of every aspect of your life, and the skills that you learn now will only help you in the future.

Also, availability of information has grown at astronomical rates just in the past few decades. Today's teens are dealing with significantly higher information

How a Cell Phone Can Become a Porsche

Steven Ortiz, a California teen, was just 15 when he started trading things on Craigslist's barter site. He started with an old cell phone, moved through dirt bikes, laptops, even a golf cart, until he ended up with a 1975 Ford Bronco, a car that is considered a classic and therefore gave him enough bartering power to acquire a Porsche.

"A lot of people don't have money right now, in this economy. So they think, 'I really need a new phone, but I don't have the money. Here I have this CD player lying around that I don't use anymore, maybe I can trade,'" said Steven's father in an interview with the *San Gabriel Valley Tribune*.

It's not as simple as it sounds. Ortiz spends 5 to 6 hours per day searching online for deals and usually spends months looking for a trade for what he has on hand. It took him 2 years to get to the Porsche. According to the *Tribune* article, "'People just make these trades,' Steven said. 'I am not lying to anyone.' [Steven's father] has stressed the value of honesty in such transactions and not to take advantage of anyone."[20]

overload than their parents, yet teens are handling the challenge better than any other generation. The reason is that they have never known anything different and have already developed the coping skills that adults are still struggling to find.

How This Book Works

Our society is growing and changing with each generation, and the ability to soar on the information highway is an important tool. Congratulations for being in the generation that will alter our culture in fundamental ways!

This book covers various ways that you can interact with others via the Internet and social media sites. Each chapter focuses on a certain activity that you can do online, providing tips and hints to figure out how to make it work on your own. Because websites change as users find new ways to take advantage of what the site has to offer, this explanation will likely be very vague. It would not be helpful to you if I said that the button you need is in the top left corner if it turns out it is on the right side instead. Rather, I have included information that should assist you in finding the button and then knowing how to use it.

In addition to changing the function and appearance of websites, the sites themselves often come and go. As of this writing in 2011, MySpace is falling in popularity and may cease to exist altogether in the foreseeable future. Therefore, it is rarely mentioned in the text. It is also very likely that the site you need the most help with didn't even exist as I wrote this book and therefore isn't discussed. When branching out into new sites you have never used before, keep in mind that the basic functions of all websites are usually similar. If you are comfortable with one site, you can likely figure out the next one. Be confident in your skills and jump right in!

Notes

1. Darcy DiNucci, "Fragmented Future," *Print* 53, no. 4 (July/August 1999): 32.
2. Melissa Healy, "Teenage Social Media Butterflies May Not Be Such a Bad Idea," *Los Angeles Times*, May 18, 2010, http://articles.latimes.com/2010/may/18/science/la-sci-socially-connected-kids-20100518/2.
3. ROIWorld, "Teens and Social Networks Study," June 2010, www.scribd.com/doc/33751159/Teens-Social-Networks-Study-June-2010.
4. Amanda Lenhart et al., "Social Media and Young Adults," February 3, 2010, www.pewInternet.org/Reports/2010/Social-Media-and-Young-Adults/Part-3/1-Teens-and-online-social-networks.aspx.
5. Healy, "Teenage Social Media Butterflies."
6. Healy, "Teenage Social Media Butterflies."
7. Alicia Stetzer and Stephna May, "Teen Social Media Influencers Wield Power Online and Offline," *Ketchum*, May 25, 2010, http://newsroom.ketchum.com/news-releases/teen-social-media-Influencers-wield-power-online-and-offline.
8. Mizuko Ito et al., "Living and Learning with New Media: Summary of Findings from the Digital Youth Project," November 2008, http://digitalyouth.ischool.berkeley.edu/files/report/digitalyouth-WhitePaper.pdf.

9. Internet Safety Technical Task Force, "Enhancing Child Safety and Online Technologies," December 31, 2008, http://cyber.law.harvard.edu/sites/cyber.law.harvard.edu/files/ISTTF_Final_Report-Executive_Summary.pdf.

10. Carlos Castillo, "Get Over It: Txt Language May Be with Us 4evr," *The Record*, June 2, 2009, L-2.

11. Nicole Luth, "Texting's Shortcuts Endanger English," *The Record*, June 9, 2009, L-2.

12. Kyle Good and Sara Sinek, "New Study on Reading in the Digital Age: Parents Say Electronic, Digital Devices Negatively Affects Kids' Reading Time," *Scholastic*, September 29, 2010, http://mediaroom.scholastic.com/node/378.

13. Jacqui Cheng, "Study Confirms TXT SPK Doesn't Hurt Kids' Language Skills," *ARS Technica*, 2009, http://arstechnica.com/gadgets/news/2009/02/study-confirms-txt-spk-doesnt-hurt-kids-language-skills.ars.

14. Sheelah M. Sweeny, "Writing for the Instant Messaging and Text Messaging Generation: Using New Literacies to Support Writing Instruction," *Journal of Adolescent and Adult Literacy* 54, no. 2 (October 2010): 128.

15. Tamar Levin, "Teenagers' Internet Socializing Not a Bad Thing," *New York Times*, November 19, 2008, www.nytimes.com/2008/11/20/us/20Internet.html?_r=1.

16. Chris Hoofnagle et al., "How Different Are Young Adults from Older Adults When It Comes to Information Privacy Attitudes and Policies?" April 14, 2010, http://papers.ssrn.com/sol3/papers.cfm?abstract_id=1589864.

17. Louise Story, "Company Will Monitor Phone Calls to Tailor Ads," *New York Times*, September 24, 2007, www.nytimes.com/2007/09/24/business/media/24adcol.html?_r=1.

18. Mary Madden and Aaron Smith, "Reputation Management and Social Media," May 26, 2010, http://www.pewInternet.org/Reports/2010/Reputation-Management.aspx.

19. Larry Magid, "Study Has Good News about Kids' Online Behavior," June 22, 2010, http://news.cnet.com/8301-19518_3-20008402-238.html.

20. Rebecca Kimitch, "Glendora Teen Swaps Old Cell Phone for Porsche on Craigslist," *San Gabriel Valley Tribune*, July 16, 2010, www.sgvtribune.com/ci_15533701.

2

STAY SAFE AND BE SMART

....

"I feel really safe online. With all the different privacy settings it's really easy to keep your information private." —*Averill, age 18*

Staying Safe

Even the simplest thing can get out of hand on the Internet. For example, an Australian girl planning her sixteenth birthday party didn't have time to invite specific people, so she made it a public event and asked her friends to invite anyone she might have missed. The invite, which included her home address and phone number, went viral. She deleted the event after thousands of people responded, but someone else created a hacked version that had over 214,000 responses by the time the police got involved. In the end, the party was canceled, and police were there to protect the house if anyone showed up. The hacker who re-created the invite was arrested.

Any time you are on the Internet, you need to use the same safety rules that you learned as a child, even in the most mundane of activities. Being online doesn't make you safer just because the people you are interacting with are not physically present. If you make bad choices and the wrong sort of person notices, you could be in physical danger too. Each chapter in this book discusses safety and privacy measures specific to the sort of website being discussed.

This is a list of basic ground rules you should always follow:

- Never put identifying facts about yourself in a public profile—you wouldn't give your phone number or e-mail address out to some random person

What Teens Are Saying

"I do feel safe online. I know how to use security settings on Facebook and know what will create me in an unsafe situation." —Adam, age 17

"I feel pretty safe online, I don't go to chat boards or give out my information, so nobody can really 'get' me without stuff that I won't give them, so I'm safe." —Annie, age 16

"I never give my real name, address or age. Anyone who knows me can ask for my online name(s) to find me." —Ava, age 16

"I feel pretty safe online because I normally go on websites that I trust and even if I do get a virus I know how to get rid of it as I am a computer person. I use Bluecoat K9 web protection so that I don't look at any porn or any illegal website." —Daniel, age 17

you met on the street, right? Use the same common sense when giving out information online. A savvy Internet predator can put together details about your life and determine your name and address. Just don't provide those kinds of details!

- Never give away your password to anyone (except that trusted adult who oversees your Internet use).
- If you're uncomfortable with something, log off!
- Don't post hurtful messages about other people. Your actions online may have consequences offline.
- It's never funny to impersonate someone else. In fact, it can be dangerous.
- Always remember that the Internet is permanent. If you post it, it will always be there even if you want to take it down later. An embarrassing picture can be spread to other websites in less than a second.

"I feel very safe. I have never had a problem online that I couldn't just ignore or walk away from." —Jack C., age 14

"I feel fairly safe online, I don't feel like I have any reason not to. I keep any profiles I have on the private setting, and I don't accept friend requests from people I don't know personally. Not that I've been in this sort of situation, but if I did start to feel unsafe, I'd let my parents know and delete whatever account I was being harassed on. But I'd rather focus on prevention rather than recovery." —Niki, age 15

"I feel fine online, I usually don't talk to people I don't like and I'm pretty computer literate so I know what I'm doing around a keyboard. I think that more often then not, when people are targeted for online predators or malicious hackers, it's because they're either ignorant or not well educated enough to know how to defend themselves." —Bow, age 20

"Unfortunately, not very safe. I don't give out my personal information." —Jake, age 13

- Don't give clues about your whereabouts. If you have details about your home in your public profile and then publish a status update about being out of town, you are inviting bad people to break into your house. If you think that details such as where you live are already public, you can keep yourself safe by not giving current information that could be used to track your movements. It's okay to give a city (except if you live in a really small town!). Refer to places with generic names, such as "school" or "club."

- If you're in trouble—as if someone is repeatedly making you feel uncomfortable or if you are worried about your privacy—talk to a parent or other trusted adult. It's their job to help keep you safe, and they can do a better job if you confide in them, even if it's horribly embarrassing!

Identifying Facts

- Your full name
- Anything that has a number: your age, birth date, e-mail address, or phone numbers
- Where you can be found, including home address, school name, or favorite hangout place
- Family facts—such as where your parents work, how much they paid for the new car, ages of your siblings, where your grandmother lives, or even your grades

- Pay attention to age limits—websites that require registration will have age limit rules. They have that rule for a reason; don't pretend to be older just to get on the site.

- Protect your computer—don't go to websites that you know will result in a virus! These are the more sketchy websites that may make you uncomfortable.

- Never arrange a real-life meeting with a stranger you meet online without first discussing the idea with your trusted adults and arranging for a public group meeting. Someone who insists that you come alone could be a predator.

- Use the site's privacy features—check under "account settings" for privacy settings. Most social networks will allow you to limit your profile to only friends, which keeps the strangers from learning anything about you. Check those privacy settings frequently, as they may change with little or no notice.

Most of all, trust your instincts. You are not required to share anything! Make wise choices about what you do share. You learned how to be safe when you were a child, and those rules still apply online. If your gut tells you something is wrong, protect yourself no matter how embarrassing it is. That goes for crossing the

> ### Children's Online Privacy Protection Act of 1998
>
> Why do so many websites say that you have to be 13 to be a member? Because it's just easier for them to comply with the Children's Online Privacy Protection Act. This federal law says that websites must follow special rules when collecting information from a child under the age of 13, sometimes including parental consent. Many websites have decided to discourage children from joining their websites rather than deal with the paperwork and potential fines for allowing them.

street to not walk by someone you are afraid of, as well as closing a chat room when another user is rude.

It Can't Be *That* Bad, Right?

"I can tell you from experience that there are a lot of bad things on the Internet. I would advise all teenagers to avoid bad websites and videos. They will mess you up." —Jake, age 13

The majority of teens on the Internet will be safe online and never have any serious problems. But it could be anyone, including you, who gets into trouble over what seems like a perfectly safe situation.

> ### Facebook Has Different Privacy Settings for Minors
>
> If you're under 18, Facebook automatically sets your page private for everyone except friends, friends of friends, and those in your networks. This happens even when you have your privacy settings on "everyone." But when you turn 18, it changes! Be sure to check on your privacy settings before your birthday.

What Teens Are Saying

"I have my settings set so no one can see anything except my name and my picture unless they are my friends." —Priyanka, age 15

"I am extremely paranoid about privacy, so I keep up with the FaceSpace's updates about that stuff, but I would say that some of my friends are not as vigilant." —Ava, age 16

"Every once in a while I check my Facebook settings to make sure they're still on private and that nothing's changed too much. Perhaps other teens ignore privacy settings but I keep tabs on them—again, just to make sure I still feel safe enough." —Niki, age 15

"I simply set all my privacy settings so that nobody can get any information about me, unless they are someone I know. And I never put information that strangers shouldn't know anyway. I feel that even if I had low privacy settings, people couldn't get too much information about me." —Annie, age 16

"It is true that the settings change, but the major important ones don't, and as long as you take five minutes to look over them every few months you're not going to have an issue. Some kids, though, have their privacy settings so high that you can't even friend request them, and I think that's great if that's the level of security that makes them comfortable." —Averill, age 18

"Oh I know that teens don't give a monkey about their privacy, especially on FB, I mean you can easily go on someone's FB and look at where they live, how old they are, look at their parents, pictures and such. I pay a lot of attention to it; I mostly pay attention to the birth date." —Daniel, age 17

People Who Might Be Reading Your Profile

In addition to your friends, there are others who might look for your profile:

- Parents and siblings
- Other family members, such as grandparents, aunts, uncles, or cousins
- Friends' parents
- Teachers and other school officials
- Potential employers
- Coworkers
- College officials
- Reporters
- Internet predators

Take Ashleigh Hall, for instance. This British 17-year-old was kidnapped, raped, and murdered by Peter Chapman, a 33-year-old sex offender, who approached her on Facebook using the stolen identity of a 19-year-old man. Chapman lured Ashleigh away for an overnight visit after just 6 days of chatting. It is unknown how he became Ashleigh's friend on Facebook, as none of her friends knew about him. Chapman's fake profile had hundreds of teen girls in his friends list, and in an interview with the *Daily Mail*, Ashleigh's mother said, "He told her she was lovely, funny and pretty."[1] She continues to speak out about safety measures on Facebook.

So What *Can* You Share?

"Don't use your phone in excess, be careful when talking to strangers—though good things can come from it, never let netspeak overpower correct grammar and don't send photos you wouldn't want your mother to see." —Grace, age 16

❓ What Does Facebook Block?

All social media sites pay close attention to illegal activities on their site. Facebook has a "hate and harassment team" that does nothing but remove offensive posts. While some things are missed, it does focus on the major issues. If the post is illegal either by law or by Facebook's terms of service, it is removed. If you come across something that offends you on Facebook, click the "report" button. The team will look into it . . . eventually.

It's always fine to share about general interests, such as bands, sports, movies, and TV shows. It's also always fine to share how you feel about something, especially if you leave out identifying parts, like names and places.

POS: Parent over Shoulder

Work with your parents and other trusted adults to keep yourself safe online. Many parents are really worried about what you might run into out there in the world and, especially if they are not net savvy themselves, may fear the Internet. (Check out teachparentstech.com for assistance.)

Many experts on how to keep children safe online are suggesting that parents create a profile on the site that their child uses, and one study showed that 72 percent of parents surveyed monitor their teens' social networking accounts, 50 percent of them on a weekly basis. Meanwhile, various studies have shown that

- more than half of teens surveyed had parents on Facebook and some of them were leaving the site because of it,
- nearly a third of Facebook teens were ready to unfriend their parent, and
- 80 percent of teens use privacy settings to hide content from parents or certain friends.

Your parents can help you stay safe online.

Also,

- the majority of teens would turn to a parent for advice and support if they felt threatened while online, and
- almost half of children polled for one survey thought they were more careful online than their parents!

Ultimately, it is your parents' responsibility to monitor your Internet use and to make sure that you are safe. Here are some tips on how you can work with your parents so that they can be a part of your online world:

- Parents should learn about your favorite websites firsthand. Offer to assist them in setting up a profile and be open about your feelings of them seeing your posts. A little bit of knowledge will go a long way to addressing their fears.
- Discuss what information they are comfortable with you sharing online and why they feel that way. Respect their wishes.

What Teens Are Saying

"I honestly think there is the threat of meeting strangers online who want to hurt you but if you pay any attention at all they are pretty easy to see before they get anywhere, so keep your security settings up and be careful but don't forget to have fun." —Jack S., age 17

"I believe in the general rule of 'stranger danger!' that we all learn in kindergarten. I only chat with people on online gaming sites and never give out my personal information." —Jack C., age 14

"I interact with strangers if only through gaming sites. I never give out any real information and never meet them in real life." —Adam, age 17

"Kids meeting strangers doesn't seem safe to me. I don't 'friend' people I don't know in the real(er) world." —Ava, age 16

"I recently joined my college's class of 2015 page on Facebook that's just for all the accepted students to see who each other is before we actually meet in August. This is the first time that I've ever really talked to strangers online, but this is obviously a controlled setting. It's a private group managed by admissions, so you know everyone there is actually going to be in your class. I've chatted with a few people and friended some more, but I feel like there is some basis of knowing them beyond pure stranger." —Averill, age 18

"I was part of an alpha testing team and everyone there was a stranger to me and everyone was strangers to each other. Yet everyone on there was and is extremely nice. Most of the people on there are adults, I was the youngest person on there. I met this one person, her name is Anne. I met her in real life, because she was passing through where I lived and so we organized that she could come by and meet me. It was fun. She is a very kind person. She came with her husband, very nice people. They only stayed for about 20 minutes, but it was fun to see someone that I had met online in real life." —Daniel, age 17

"There was a guy and girl, both 14ish, chatting online. They were actually who they said they were, but both of their dads thought the other was a perv waiting to strike. So the dads start chatting and when they eventually met in person, the dads argued while the kids hung out." —Jack C., age 14

"I don't really interact with strangers [except] the ones my friends know, and only with reasons." —Priyanka, age 15

"I do interact with strangers online as I play many MMO games. I meet them through the game and I usually keep our relationship restricted to the game. If I feel comfortable enough with a person I'll add them to a social networking site, such as Facebook, and go from there. It's all about steps and systems. For an example, I met a family from Pennsylvania about six years ago through World of Warcraft. I slowly started to get to know them and eventually we became really close real life friends." —Bow, age 20

"If I was going to meet someone, though, I'd make sure it was in a busy place with people I know and trust around me, of course!" —Niki, age 15

- Assure your parents that you are using very secure passwords, which you do not share with anyone other than them.
- Ask them to help you prioritize your time online versus time for your homework, family, friends, and other real-world activities. Help them understand how you can do multiple tasks at once and how you take that into account in your decision making.
- If your parents are concerned about a certain site, suggest that they contact the people who run the site to get answers to their questions. Find contact information in the help pages or at the bottom of the main page.
- Ask your parent to install Internet security on your computer. Do your part by not downloading risky files that could infect the computer.

What Teens Are Saying

"Occasionally my parents will look at my online history, but they don't do any more than that (or at least not that I know about . . .). They used to hover over my shoulder, but I've convinced them that I have the responsibility to not do anything stupid that I would regret, and they loosened up. And I've definitely held up my end of the bargain!" —Niki, age 15

"My parents have practically no involvement with the computer and me. I think it is because they trust me and because the computers are in the family room." —Daniel, age 17

"[My parents] always have to have my password for my e-mail, gets annoying." —Jack C., age 14

"[My parents] monitor [my Internet use] a lot. I can't get away with anything. I felt kind of annoyed, but safe." —Jake, age 13

"I think that parents need to be more mindful of who their teens are talking to." —Bow, age 20

"I think texting allows people to talk about things that might be hard to talk about face to face. Like how to actually talk to each other." —Annie, age 16

- Explain the research that has shown that teens behave the same way online as they do offline. Point out how you are responsible in the real world, so they can be assured you will behave the same way online. Give them examples.
- Discuss how your parents will respect your personal boundaries. Where those boundaries lie depend on your age, maturity, and whether you have earned their trust with previous behavior.

- Sometimes you will innocently find something on the Internet that upsets or embarrasses you. It is not your fault that this happened! Talk to your parents about these situations, and let them know how they can help you process such situations.
- If your parents set limits on your social network time that you feel are inappropriate, discuss your concerns with them and provide examples of why you disagree. Have possible solutions ready to suggest, and be flexible about finding a compromise. Respectful communication of your concerns will get you a lot further than a tantrum!

If applicable, talk to your parents about how they are not protecting you as well as you would like. Let them know what they could do better in supporting you.

Your parents have instilled their values in you since you were born. Help them to understand that you are trustworthy, by behaving responsibly and by talking to them about what you do online. That doesn't mean you must friend your mom on Facebook! Just take the time to show her your profile and answer her questions. The more time you spend showing them that you are making good decisions, the more they will trust you to go it alone.

Consider creating a contract regarding Internet use with your parents. Together, you and your parents can decide what the rules will be, and you can write them down so that they are clear to everyone. Prepare for the conversation by making a list of what you enjoy doing online as well as what you would like to be doing, and think about why you enjoy doing the things you do.

The contract could include details such as

- Time limits for typical, daily use
- Whether Internet use for homework or extracurricular projects counts toward time limits
- Sites and activities you are allowed to use and perform
- Sites and activities you will not use and perform
- Internet use when you're home alone
- Internet use outside of the home, as in school, the library, or a friend's house

- How you will protect your privacy and be safe
- How you will protect your reputation
- How you will tell your parent if something uncomfortable or dangerous has happened to you
- Strategies to determine where Internet use fits into your priorities, including homework, time with family, time with friends, and other interests
- A promise that you will make responsible choices
- The consequences for not following the rules

Your contract should also include how your parent will be involved.[2] Here are some requests you may want to make:

- Help keep you safe online.
- Respect the knowledge and skills you will learn.
- Pay attention to what you're doing online and discuss problems, including how they will respond if you come to them with a concern.
- Assist you in setting privacy settings.
- Respect your privacy unless there are significant reasons for concern.
- Not overreact; be respectful in how they express concerns.
- Explain the reasoning behind any decisions, including restrictions.

You can also search online for "Internet use agreement" for samples to get you started.

Extreme Privacy

You may want to use a site but not want to put anything about yourself on it. You can usually create a profile with a fake name or a nickname. Plan ahead if you're going to do this, as many social media sites won't let you change your name later. You control how much information you put on the site, so choose to not post anything you aren't comfortable with.

The bigger issue is controlling what your friends post on your profile. You can delete posts that other people leave for you. Some teens delete literally everything on their profile each time they log out. Others go so far as to deactivate the account each time they log out and then reactivate it when they return. That makes it so no one can see or add to your page when you aren't logged in.

How to Google Yourself

"Think about the reality of your information online. Information about you is already available in many places, so you need to remain aware of the whole picture in order to keep yourself, your friends and your family safe."[3]—Angela Alcorn in "The Very Unofficial Facebook Privacy Manual"

It's important to be aware of what is said about you online to protect your privacy and your reputation. You can also find information on a person you just met in this manner.

Search for your name in Google or another search engine. Here are some hints:

- Put quotes around your full name so that it is searched as a single term instead of separate words—for example, "John Doe."
- Search for your e-mail addresses, phone numbers, or any nicknames.
- Use specific search engines, such as Google's news and blogs searches.

If you find something that you want removed, there are a few things to do. This can be very difficult!

- If it's a site that you created, go there and delete the content. Find the delete account option and use it.
- Contact the site's owner and request that he or she remove the information or page. Check the "contact us" or "help" page to find out how.
- Request that the information be corrected so that it is accurate. Do so by contacting the site owner and including a suggestion to replace the statement.
- Ask the search engine to remove the page. Check its help page to find out how.
- If you are under the age of 13, the Federal Trade Commission (www.ftc.gov) can require that the information be removed because of the Children's

Online Privacy Protection Act. Your parent needs to contact the commission to file a complaint.

- If the information that you found could cause physical harm, contact the police. This includes, for example, your phone number or address or any suggestion of sexual solicitation or harassment.

Passwords

"I know that it probably is not a smart idea to give out my password, but it can be really hard not to when someone that you trust implicitly—at least at the time—asks you for your password for a legitimate reason that really won't have any effect on you." —Jade, age 18

You know to never, ever share your password, not even with your best friend. Sometimes it can be difficult, as Jade explains. If you really feel the need to give a friend your password, change it to something generic or unique and then change it back when the friend is finished.

Do you know how to make a good, secure password? The goal is to protect your online presence while having a password that you can actually remember. Never use a password that contains a part of your name, something you enjoy doing, pets, birth date, or another word people could guess if they know you.

The more complicated your password, the less likely it is to be broken. Hackers have programs that can guess at passwords very quickly. Table 2.1 shows the speed with which a hacker using a network of multiple computers can hack an 8-digit password.[4]

The best way to create a password is to have a sentence you remember easily and then make initials out of it. For instance, "I attended King Middle School in 2005" could become "IaKMSi05." Then change at least one of the letters to a symbol, like making the capital I into an exclamation point: "!aKMSi05." This password combines symbols, numbers, and both upper- and lowercase letters, making it a very secure password.

Table 2.1. Time It Takes to Hack a Password

Type of password	Time to hack
Numbers	Instant
All lowercase or all uppercase letters	6 hours
Upper- and lowercase letters mixed	6 days
Mixed upper- and lowercase letters, plus numbers	25.5 days
Mixed upper- and lowercase letters, plus common symbols	346 days
Mixed upper- and lowercase letters, numbers, and common symbols	2.25 years

It is also a good idea to have a very long password. You can make any password longer by repeating it once or even twice. The more digits involved, the longer it will take to hack it. Even a very simple password is difficult to crack if it is long enough. In the case of table 2.1, a hacker with a network of computers would take 6.3 trillion years to hack a 20-digit password of just lowercase letters. Imagine how long it would take to crack a 20-digit password of mixed letters, numbers, and symbols!

You should have a different password for each site you log in to. This is a pain, but it is the surest way to protect yourself. If you use the same password everywhere, one could be hacked, and then all of them are hacked, even if it is the best password ever. Consider making your sentence something uniform, and then change the name of the site in each password. For instance, "I really enjoy<whatever>in 2010" would be shortening to "IreFi2010" for Facebook, "IreGi2010" for Google, and "IreWPi2010" for WordPress.

Now that you have all of these really good passwords, you will have to remember them. It's okay to write down your passwords as long as you keep them in a very safe location—meaning not in your computer or phone and not where anyone who is in your room can see them. Write them down with a pen—even typing them into a document on your computer can compromise your passwords.

It's also very wise to change your passwords on a regular basis. How often you do it depends on how secure you feel about your passwords, but do it at least once or twice a year. Yes, it's a pain, but it's your online identity at stake!

Romance (and Friendship) in the Online World

Being behind a computer monitor gives you a sense of security and therefore makes a new relationship much easier to begin. There are no awkward pauses or clammy palms to suffer through. A lot of people are finding love online. In fact, one online dating site study found that 2.57 percent of couples marrying in the United States met on its site.

Social media sites make it easier for you to get to know your crush. *Seventeen Magazine* did a survey about the role of Facebook in teen romance. It found that 60 percent of teens check out their crush's site daily and 72 percent felt that talking online brought them closer to a new friend in real life. Furthermore, 43 percent of girls and 33 percent of boys admitted that they would not date someone solely on the basis of his or her Facebook profile. Also, 10 percent of teens have been dumped via Facebook, and 27 percent removed their ex from their regular screens after the breakup.

We've all done it. You meet someone new and take a thorough look at his or her Facebook profile. The person has no idea that anyone has looked, and you may learn something juicy. You may also find something interesting that you can use to start a conversation the next time you're talking.

Amy Summers, teen columnist for socialtimes.com, says, "I would estimate that every single person with a social networking account has participated in this activity at some stage. Natural curiosity has driven us to gossip for centuries, so

What Teens Are Saying

"There was this one site, and people kept asking if I liked them. We were using avatars, so they only like how my avatar looked." —Jake, age 13

"I haven't had any online relationships, and I'm not a fan of the idea. Talking to someone online is much different than talking to them face-to-face, and it's easier to type than to say something out loud. I'd rather have someone I'm comfortable talking to in real life." —Niki, age 15

"I currently am in a long-distance relationship that is maintained through frequent visits, texts and online communication. It's hard but the evolution of the Internet and technology has made it easier." —Bow, age 20

"I knew some girls online from Facebook via some of my other friends, and we started to talk, we have never met in real life, but they were proper pushing a relationship." —Daniel, age 17

"I have made friends on a game I play, but as far as an actual relationship, neither online or offline. My advice is meet in person." —Jack C., age 14

it comes as no surprise that as technology advances, so do our tools for digging around in the lives of others."[5] It's called *Facebook stalking*, and it is a normal part of online life. But is it creepy? It can be!

Keep it from being creepy by limiting how much time you spend on it. Keeping a close eye on what your crush posts is very different from obsessively scouring the profile of someone you wouldn't talk to in real life. Be aware of how much of your time is spent secretly watching people in a way you wouldn't want to admit to their faces. If it would make you uncomfortable for someone else to be watching you that way, it's probably not okay for you to do it to them.

Use social media to check out your crush.

Here are some tips for developing online relationships, both romantic and friend:

- Watch your intensity level—there is no need to rush! Take it slow, and don't overwhelm the other person (or yourself) with constant contact. It's normal to be excited and antsy to see someone online, just as when you meet a new person in real life, but don't go overboard. You may not notice how many times you've sent messages, but the person will notice when dealing with a full in-box!

- Just as when meeting a new person in real life, you don't know everything about him or her right away or even quickly. Remember that all the information you have about an online friend is through your text conversations and a profile page. A person may be very talkative and sensitive online but can barely put 2 words together in person. Pictures can be altered or taken from flattering angles. It's best to keep an open mind about a new friend and remember that there is more to him or her than what is shown on a website.

- Online relationships are considerably more risky than real-life ones because expectations can be built up and then not justified. Also, life happens extra fast in the online world, and a relationship that might stay exciting for a month or more in real life could last only a week online. Protect yourself by not expecting too much, too soon.

- If it's a serious relationship, can it happen only online? Yes, it's possible, but is it a good idea? If you consider your online friend, especially if it's a romance, to be "serious" even though you've never met him or her, there may be a problem. Relationships are about being able to get along in real life as well as online, so don't get too serious until you know you can do both.

Steps for Taking an Online Romance into the Real World

- Be safe! Do your best to make sure that the people you're talking to online are who they say they are. If you have a mutual friend, ask him or her about this person.

- Talk to your parents about the new friend. Ask for advice in contacting this person safely.

- Use private chat, instant messaging, or e-mail to communicate outside the eyes of the world.

- Exchange phone numbers. Only do this step when you really believe that your new friend is a good person and has portrayed himself or herself as he or she really is. Phone numbers can give more information, including where you live! A phone conversation is a safe way to get to know a person in a much more real way.

- Meet in person in a public place with a good friend or parent along. Never go alone to meet an online friend in real life, no matter how much you trust him or her.

When to Change Your Relationship Status

Never change your relationship status on your profile without talking with the other person about it first. Imagine how it would feel if you got home from a great first date and did a little stalking on the person's social network of choice (because, of course, you talked about that on the date) and see that the site lists him or her as "in a relationship." Would you assume that the friend meant you, or is that person cheating on someone? And what if your date did get home and immediately changed his or her status to show a relationship? That's more than a little creepy.

Either way, it's best to wait until you've had the talk and to both change your relationship status at the same time. Instead, put an update out there about how you're feeling. Your friends want the details, and your date will be flattered.

What Teens Are Saying

"I believe it's alright to talk to people online that you haven't met in person, but everyone should be careful what they say, and be sure of the person they are talking to. Never arrange to meet someone from the Internet unless you are 100 percent sure they are who they say they are, and don't go alone as a precaution." —Grace, age 16

"I think online dating is tricky with teens. Setting aside safety concerns, I think most teenagers usually depend a lot on the relationships that surround them in real life. When you start accepting 'cute strangers' into your life just like all the other friends you know, I think it can be problematic. If you never meet the person (or even if you do only once or twice), there are certain ways you can never know them in the same way you know the friends you interact with in person every day. So knowing whether the relationship would actually work offline, or if the person is even loyal to you, is very hard to figure out. It's an old game with new rules: you can calculate how much the other teen is 'into you' by how many times their name pops up to talk to you on chat, how many hearts they use to sign off their Facebook messages, how many photos they 'liked' of you."[6] —Caroline, 11th grade, on YPulse.com

---

Evaluating What You Find on the Internet

The web is accessible for anyone who has a way to connect a computer to the Internet. People can put up anything they want. All they have to do is buy a domain name and upload their own websites. For that reason, it is safest to not trust anything you find online. When you're just surfing, that's not such a big deal, but if you're looking up something important—for an assignment or for personal information—the Internet is just one place to find information. It is a good idea to verify whatever you find online in a reputable source, such as a book or subscription database.

However, some websites are trustworthy, or sometimes you have to go with an Internet source because nothing else is current, complete, or available when you need it. The following are some things to consider when you're deciding if a website is worthy of your trust.

Where Did You Find the Website?

A study of college freshmen showed that the top result in their search was deemed most useful regardless of anything else! Most search engines rank results based on popularity, putting a website that has been clicked on more toward the top. But think about how often you've clicked on the first site and found it lacking, so you go back and try another link—each one you click on counts in the overall algorithm, even if it was useless.

It is useful to know that a certain site was more popular than another, but that should be your starting point rather than your final evaluation.

Who Hosts the Website?

You can tell something about the person who owns the site from a website address. The ending of every website address gives a hint:

.com = commercial website

.org = nonprofit organization

.net = telecommunications company

.edu = educational facility

.mil = military website

.gov = government website

Unfortunately, these meanings are getting blurry. Anyone can buy a .com, .org, or .net. Educational facilities use .edu but may give space to their students and not regulate what they put up on those addresses. The military and the government, at least in the United States, do regulate what is put up on their sites; therefore, those are trustworthy.

Country Codes on Websites

Websites also tell what country they are from. With the exception of the United States, all countries must put a 2-letter code at the end of their addresses. Some US websites have the .us at the end, but it's not required. Here are some common country codes:

.uk = United Kingdom

.nl = Netherlands

.au = Australia

.de = Germany

.jp = Japan

To find out what a code means, search online for "international country codes" or just the code itself.

It's a good idea to know where the website you are loading is coming from. At the very least, load time may be affected if it's coming from the other side of the world. It can also indicate that you're getting into a website you may want to avoid; a lot of websites that are illegal in the United States have an .nl code since laws are very different in the Netherlands.

Also pay attention to the domain name of the website. This is the word before the .com ending, for instance, the "Ford" in ford.com or the "CNN" in cnn.com. If your search comes from a source that you would trust in the real world, it's likely you can trust it in the online world too. A great example of a website you can trust for medical information on cancer is the American Cancer Society's cancer .org. However, if the website is from jokewallpaper.com, it's likely not meant to be serious.

Even if the website has a good host, the length of the website address will give you a hint as well. Each slash (/) that occurs in a website indicates a subfolder. The fewer the slashes, the closer to the original site the website is; therefore, the more it is regulated by that organization. If you see a website address like this one, be wary: www.uas.alaska.edu/students/~smeyer/friends/bella/<3/edward.

Who Wrote the Website, and When Was It Posted?

A good website will have contact information for the organization at the very bottom of the page. Check there to see if someone has taken credit for the information and the copyright date. If there is no way to contact the website's creator, that's a sign that whoever put it up doesn't want to be held accountable for the content.

Consider if the website owner or author will get something out of you using the site. Some commercial sites are designed to record your clicks and pay someone for your attention. Other websites will offer good information but give the impression that their product is the best one.

How Does the Website Look? Is it Usable?

If you can't stand to look at the site, is it really a worthy source? Some websites are covered in flashing neon colors, created with text and background color in a hard-to-read combination, or are just so badly created that you can't even figure out where the information is hiding.

Also consider how the website functions. Are the links all working or mostly broken, leading to the wrong thing or to an error page? Are the advertisements so overwhelming that you can't tell what's real and what's an ad? Is it difficult to navigate or search for what you need? And when you try to leave, does it trap you or overwhelm you with pop-up ads? All of these are signs that this is a website you are better off ignoring.

What Is the Purpose of the Site?

Has it been designed for informational or commercial purposes? Which do you need for your search?

Is the Site Biased?

As you compare different sites with similar information, keep a critical eye out for discrepancies that may indicate a bias in the information. It's likely that you are looking for balanced accurate information, and you may need to compare multiple sites to be sure that you have it all.

Is the Information Confirmable?

Most of all, use your common sense when deciding to trust a website. Check multiple sources and compare the information. Use the information obtained from a search database through your school or public library's website, since those are as good as actual published books.

Using What You Find on the Internet

There are plenty of instances where you want to steal something from the Internet and use it for your own purpose. It is very likely that anything you find online is not free and that you're breaking the law if you take it. This law is called *copyright*, and it says that anything published in any format is owned by the creator and cannot be used without permission. How would you feel if a classmate published a blog that you wrote in the school newspaper as his or her own writing? Your blog is covered by copyright; therefore, this student would have broken the copyright law. (If this happens to you, report it to a school administrator immediately!) There are complicated exceptions about legally using copyrighted materials for

Test Your Evaluation Skills

Think you can tell a good website from a bad one? Take a look at these websites and decide your opinion before reading the explanations.

Pacific Northwest Tree Octopus: http://zapatopi.net/treeoctopus/. Nice website, isn't it? Did it occur to you that an octopus really couldn't live out of the water? This website is a hoax!

Dog Island: www.thedogisland.com. Would your dog love to run free for the rest of its life? Did you notice that the service is free? It's also not real. Scroll down to the very bottom and click on "disclaimer" for the real story.

Mankato, Minnesota, tourist wonderland: http://city-mankato.us/. Minnesota is on the northern edge of the United States, and common sense tells us that it's unlikely to be at least 70 degrees year-round. Again, check the disclaimer at the very bottom.

Supernatural Registration Authority: http://monsterlicenses.com/index.php. This site is professional looking and meets all of our criteria except confirming the information found there. Click on the privacy policy at the bottom of the page for details.

educational purposes. Ask your teacher for help if your project is for school.

While many instances of this kind of theft are harmless and may never be caught, it's still not a good idea. Consider the moral implications of stealing just because it's easy—is that something you want to know about yourself? There are places online that provide photos, music, and information for free.

Creative Commons is a free alternative to copyright. It gives owners of creative works the right to allow people to use, post, or even alter their art legally. That means that you can legally borrow a picture for a homework assignment or even personal use.

Watch for the following symbols to know what is permissible. Learn more about Creative Commons at http://creativecommons.org/.[7]

> ⚠️ **Copyright**
>
> 🔘 To learn more about copyright, visit this explanation from the Library of Congress: www.loc.gov/teachers /copyrightmystery/.

Attribution: You let others copy, distribute, display, and perform your copyrighted work—and derivative works based on it—but only if they give credit the way you request.

ShareAlike: You allow others to distribute derivative works only under a license identical to the license that governs your work.

NonCommercial: You let others copy, distribute, display, and perform your work—and derivative works based on it—but for noncommercial purposes only.

NoDerivs: You let others copy, distribute, display, and perform only verbatim copies of your work, not derivative works based on it.

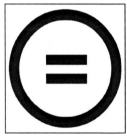

Creative Commons symbols: Attribution, ShareAlike, NonCommercial, and No Derivs.

In plain English, *Attribution* means that you can use it but that you need to cite your source, which will tell you how to do that. *ShareAlike* means that you can use it but that you must give the same Creative Commons license to your work for others to use. *NonCommercial* means that you can use it as long as you don't make money from it. Finally, *NoDerivs* means that you can use it as long as you don't alter it in any way. Altering may be as simple as making a color photo into black and white or as complex as a parody on the story.

Follow the guidelines set out by the owner of the work when you use it, and be sure to put your own guidelines on your published work to benefit others.

"Help! It Won't Close!" Or, the Power of Alt-F4 and Control-Q

No matter how safe you're being, you will probably run into something you don't want to see. The first thing to do is to close the screen. Don't panic, just click the x and get out of there.

But sometimes that doesn't work! Many sites that are intrusive, especially pornography, will have little programs running behind a website that effectively trap you on their site. If you click on the x to close or on the "exit" option and another screen pops up, that's called "mouse trapping." No matter where you click, it will see that as an invitation to open another screen you don't want! Also, some websites are written to ignore your clicking on any of the usual exits, a trick called "page jacking."

The best way to deal with anything like this is a keyboard shortcut. Since these programs run on mouse clicks, they can be solved by not using the mouse. In Microsoft Windows, hold down the Alt key and push the F4 button. On a Mac, hold down the Control button and push Q (for quit). These keyboard shortcuts close whatever screen is active at the time. It won't hurt your computer, but it will close that program right away!

Notes

1. Frances Hardy, "Failed by the Police. Failed by Facebook. A Family Torn Apart by the Cunning of an Online Predator," *Daily Mail*, November 1, 2010, www.dailymail.co.uk/fe-mail/article-1323439/Failed-Facebook-police-Ashleigh-Halls-family-torn-apart-online-predator.html.
2. Nancy E. Willard, *Cyber-Safe Kids, Cyber-Savvy Teens* (San Francisco: Jossey-Bass, 2007), 299.
3. Angela Alcorn, "The (Very) Unofficial Facebook Privacy Manual," n.d., www.scribd.com/doc/39495302/The-Very-Unofficial-Facebook-Privacy-Manual.
4. LockDown, "Password Recovery Speeds," July 10, 2009, www.lockdown.co.uk/?pg=combi.
5. Amy Summers, "A Teen Speaks: Do We Even Want to See Who's Looking at Our Facebook

Pages?" *Social Times*, March 9, 2011, http://socialtimes.com/a-teen-speaks-do-we-even-want-to-see-whos-looking-at-our-facebook-pages_b37430.

6. Caroline Marques, "The Blurred Lines between Online Dating and Dating Online," June 1, 2010, www.ypulse.com/a-teens-take-on-online-dating.

7. Creative Commons, "About the Licenses," http://creativecommons.org/about/licenses/. Symbols provided by Creative Commons, https://creativecommons.org/about/downloads/.

STICK UP FOR YOURSELF: CYBERBULLYING

··

"Any bullying hurts a live person." —Ava, age 16

Bullying is a major issue for many people in the online and real worlds. It is easier to be mean online because you don't have to look the person in the eye or hear his or her immediate response. Adults are increasingly concerned about how teens are behaving online. Parents often aren't as tech-savvy as their teens, and they don't understand how the online world works. Parents want to protect their children from harm.

Not all conflict is bullying. Everyone deals with conflict; it is a natural part of life. If that conflict is between 2 people with equal stakes in the situation, it is likely to be solved through normal avenues and does not leave lasting harm. Jade, talking about her school, said, "Of course there was a fair share of gossip, but I would argue that that is a bit different than just bullying in and of itself." Bullying is when the parties involved are not equal and there is lasting harm.

Cyberbullying is defined various ways by different researchers. The common thread is that it is intentionally harmful behavior that is done repeatedly through electronic devices such as the Internet and phone. Note that this means that the behavior has happened more than once and is done on purpose with intent to harm. Bullying in the real world can blow over in a few days

Cyberbullying can spill over into real life.

or even hours, but cyberbullying sticks around because everything online is there forever.

How Often Is Bullying Happening?

Measuring cyberbulling is difficult. Studies on the topic provide a variety of statistics. One 2010 survey, done by McAfee, found that only 29 percent of teens have experienced cyberbullying and only 11 percent admit to bullying another person, but 52 percent said that they knew someone who was involved in a bullying situation. Other studies done between 2000 and 2010 found that cyberbullying victims range from 6 to 43 percent of the surveyed teens.

It does appear that cyberbullying is happening much less often than what the media reports. A study by the Crimes against Children Research Center found

What Teens Are Saying

"Bullying is going to happen everywhere, people (particularly children) seem to be addicted to being cruel to others. Social networking should not replace face-to-face talking." —Ava, age 16

"I used to play Runescape and on these games, when you bully or say something that isn't good then you can get reported and banned from that game. I think that this embeds a couple rules into gamers' heads who play these kind of games that not saying nice stuff isn't good." —Daniel, age 17

"With the gaming sites I'm on, you can ignore people and the like so that you don't get messages from them." —Jack C., age 14

that only 1 percent of child victimization cases involved the Internet, whereas another study recommended that online interpersonal offenses be considered bullying only when they are related to offline bullying. One cyberbullying website, cyberbully411.com, says that bullying "shouldn't be seen as 'inevitable' or 'normal teen behavior,'"[1] and it cites a study saying that only 9 percent of youth were bullied.

This lack of consistency seems to be caused by a difference in opinion about what bullying looks like between the teens who live with it and the adults who research it. Social media researcher danah boyd found that teens think that bullying is when the victim doesn't deserve it, whereas things like rumors, gossip, and even physical fighting are deserved on the basis of previous incidents. Adults, however, see all of these behaviors as bullying.

The good news is that 94 percent of teens feel that they know how to be safe online. Also, only 25 percent said that they wouldn't know what to do if they are bullied, a percentage that has decreased significantly since 2008, "suggesting that teens may now be better equipped to handle cyberbullying."[2]

What Teens Are Saying

"Bullying online is a real problem, because the results and effects of the bullying are not seen." —Ariel, age 18

"One time this kid I knew made a fake e-mail account under the name of a girl I knew. He sent e-mails out to several guys saying something like 'I think you're really cute, you should ask me out.' So about 3 guys did." —Jack C., age 14

"I have received a few e-mails and such things over Facebook, and MySpace (when I was a member), which were not fun to read, but really wasn't any worse than fighting over say the phone or something." —Jade, age 18

How Cyberbullying Happens

- Harassing or hateful messages, including death threats
- Impersonating the victim, including creating a fake profile about him or her or hacking the victim's online property
- Posting information or photos about the victim
- Encouraging others to bully the victim
- Encouraging others to exclude the victim by ignoring, unfriending, or blocking him or her
- Sending porn or other offensive material to the victim
- Writing damaging posts or blogs about the victim
- Stealing the victim's password
- Tricking the victim into giving away personal information and then misusing that information
- Creating a poll about a person or people, rating appearance or implying bad behaviors
- Threatening or abusing other players in gaming or virtual worlds

- Inventing or spreading gossip, revealing secrets, playing nasty jokes
- Making fun of a person

How Does Bullying Affect Teens?

The effects of bullying are widespread and serious. The Cyberbullying Research Center has done numerous studies about how bullying affects teens. It found that cyberbully victims are more likely to have low self-esteem and consider attempting suicide. Bullied teens often have school difficulty, depression, difficulty sleeping, and chronic health problems.

Researchers have also found that students who are angry or frustrated are more likely to be bullies. Interestingly, bullies often have many of the same problems as their victims. Bullying carries into adulthood too: An estimated 25 percent of elementary school bullies will have a criminal record by the time they are 30 years old.

When bullying happens in the real world, you can usually see or hear who is doing it, and you probably have some idea why. In cyberbullying, it happens through anonymous websites, so you don't always know who is behind the attack, since it could have been passed through any number of people before it got to you. It also seems like everyone knows all about it since so many people forwarded it. This makes the attack much harder to deal with, not only in having more witnesses still spreading the attack but also not necessarily knowing the bully or his or her reasons. It also makes it much easier for someone to become a bully since it feels safer and easier when one doesn't see a victim's reaction.

Teens act emotionally without thinking things through first. The adolescent brain is still developing: the emotional part of the brain forms when you are extremely young, while the rational part of the brain is still developing throughout high school and into adulthood. You'll find yourself making bad decisions or being irresponsible without meaning to. It's the experience of these mistakes that helps your brain grow and mature and therefore helps you to be more responsible and

What Teens Are Saying

"If it starts online it would definitely come on real life too." —Priyanka, age 15

"Fights from these snarky comments can spill over into the real world, causing rifts in friendships and social issues. These things hurt, and hurt is hard to leave online, because it's totally present." —Annie, age 16

"I think that actually being bullied is much harder than anyone probably tells you, and sticking up for yourself or telling an adult can often be too hard and probably fails to work more often than not." —Jade, age 18

make better decisions. Being a bully is one of those mistakes that experience and consequences must help you understand.

Why Does Cyberbullying Happen?

Most bullying happens because the bully is angry or frustrated about a situation that the victim is involved in. But there are other reasons for bullying.

For the bully, attacking another person can be fun and entertaining. "Eighty-one percent of youth said that others cyberbully because they think it's funny."[3] The bully enjoys the attention it brings and how it relieves boredom. It can be encouraged by friends, resulting in an improved sense of friendship and self-esteem for the bully.

A study of high school students in North Carolina found that bullies are most likely the teens who are interested in attaining a higher social standing. Those at the very top of the social structure did not bully others, because it would not gain them anything and it could cost them their place at the top. Those close to the top but not yet there are the ones doing the bullying because they believe that it will help them climb the social ladder.

Bullies could also enjoy the thrill in getting someone else to deliver the actual attack, both because the victim is attacked and because the attacker has been manipulated. This happens when a group of friends all bully a victim because one member expects them to.

In the moment, the bully isn't going to think about the consequences. There is also an idea that it's okay because everyone does it. Sometimes it's a challenge, especially when it involves hacking or tricking the victim into revealing personal information.

Behind the Bullying

Emily Bazelon, a reporter for *Slate*, did an in-depth investigation of the circumstances behind the suicide of 15-year-old Phoebe Prince in 2010. Bazelon found that there was much more to the story than what the international media reports indicated. Phoebe had a troubled history before moving to her new school in South Hadley, Massachusetts. Then she had short relationships with two boys, Sean and Austin. Sean and Austin's girlfriends were spreading rumors about Phoebe and verbally attacking her both online and in real life. Soon the bullying spread to other students, and, at the peak, Phoebe killed herself.

Six students, including Sean, Austin, and their girlfriends, have been charged with civil rights violation with bodily injury. Phoebe's civil rights were violated when she was called abusive names and because the bullying interfered with her right to an education. The bodily injury drove Phoebe to suicide. Sean and Austin were also charged with statutory rape because they may have had sex with Phoebe.

Bazelon questions whether these charges are valid when the entire story has been revealed. She writes, "There is no question that some of the teenagers facing criminal charges treated Phoebe cruelly. But not all of them did. And it's hard to see how any of the kids going to trial . . . ever could have anticipated the consequences of their actions, for Phoebe or for themselves. Should we send teenagers to prison for being nasty to one another? Is it really fair to lay the burden of Phoebe's suicide on these kids?"[4]

High school senior Chelsea Bischof wrote a column for the New Jersey *Record* about Phoebe Prince. She concludes, "The only way to address cyber-bullying is for the sites' stewards to become more involved in their users' activities. Safety should be a primary concern, and the only way to ensure safety is to screen the content. Users might not agree, but it's worth it if it saves just one life."[6]

What about Free Speech?

In 1965, students in two Iowa schools decided to wear black arm bands to publicize their objections to the Vietnam War. The schools quickly adopted a policy against the arm bands, and five students were suspended. The court case went all the way to the Supreme Court, which in 1969 ruled that the First Amendment right to freedom of speech is available in schools; therefore, the teens had the right to express their opinions as long as it did not create a disturbance. This is the court case that is referenced when discussing how bullying today affects schools.

Court cases involving cyberbullying today are murky because the bullying often takes place outside of the school, yet it is through the school that the students involved know one another. Schools tend to act on situations only when the school or its teachers or officials are the victim of the bullying.

Ken Paulsen, president of the First Amendment Center, wrote an opinion piece in *USA Today* titled "Sophomoric Speech Is Free Speech, Too." He concludes, "The best legal path in these cases is to treat young people posting ugly and

"Sorry I Waited a Whopping 2 Minutes to Respond to Your IM."

Need a way to fight back? ThatsNotCool.com is a dating abuse website that provides "callout cards" that you can text or message to a friend when their behavior bothers you. The website says, "Your mobile, IM, and online accounts are all a part of you. When someone you're dating is controlling, disrespecting, or pressuring you in those spaces, *that's not cool*."[7] The slogans are often sarcastic but get the point across.

   If you're afraid that you or someone you know is in an abusive relationship, check out this site and click on the "Need help?" tab. It can help you decide if it is abusive and then what to do about it.

potentially defamatory content the way we would adults. If the content is illegal or threatening, charge them. If the content is libelous, sue them, as some teachers and principals have done. And if the content is neither criminal nor libelous, accept a provocative posting as the free speech that it is."[8]

Handling Bullying

What to Do When You Are Being Bullied

Have you been told to walk away or ignore bullying, to look at it from the bully's point of view, or, even better, to become friends with the bully? While this may have worked for previous generations dealing only in the real world, such methods are not working in the online world. It is more important to develop the skills that will help you deal with any rude person, regardless of what he or she is doing or whether it is online.

The hardest thing to do if you're being bullied is to not respond or retaliate, but it's possible that the exchange will stop if you don't fight back. The bully likely wants a reaction from you, so not giving one may end the interaction. If the bully is your friend, telling him or her that he or she is making you feel bad may also stop the problem. The person may not realize that his or her joking comments are not jokes for you. If you are comfortable with the person, it's a good idea to talk to him or her about it. Try to do so face-to-face if possible.

The most important thing is that you attempt to deal with the situation. Although you can request an apology (and accept it if you believe that it is sincere), you may not get one. You may not be able to change the bully's behavior at all. But in attempting, you are standing up for yourself and your right to be respected. If you make any attempt, even if it fails, you have done the right thing.

Block the bully: unfriend him or her on a social network or use the block feature in your IM or game. Make sure your profile doesn't allow friends of friends to see your page. "Over 70 percent of teens said that being able to block cyberbullies was the most effective method of prevention."[9] If a person is bullying you via your phone, talk to your parents about contacting the phone company to block that phone number.

Be sure to talk to a trusted adult about the situation. If you feel physically threatened, that adult can help you report it to the appropriate authorities, who can do something about it. If you aren't physically in danger, though, it's harder to handle. Your trusted adult can help you brainstorm ways to deal with the situation and decide which options are realistic and reasonable.

When talking to your trusted adult, be forthcoming about what happened. If you are vague about details, it will be difficult for the adult to assist you. Tell the adult how you felt. Also, be sure to include what you fear about talking to him or her about it, including that he or she might restrict your Internet or phone time. It may be helpful to schedule a conversation time with your adult when neither of you will be distracted. Consider asking a friend to help you figure out how to begin the conversation with your parents since having a practiced opening and explanation of the situation will make it easier.

What Teens Are Saying

"The other students figured out that I walked home and took the opportunity to teach me a lesson. To this day I don't know what they were trying to teach me. They made bullying an art form. I learned a lot from them. I learned how to take a hit, how to avoid people and that the only person you can ever truly rely on is yourself." —Ava, age 16

"Bullying has made my school experience miserable. My school didn't address bullying very well. The people who were getting bullied were getting in trouble for defending themselves, and the bullies would get off scott free. That is why I am home schooling this year." —Jake, age 13

"We did have a number of assemblies and such things regarding why bullying was bad and what we should do if we saw it or were the victims and such, but we all just sort of blew them off because they would only ever repeat what was common knowledge or just what we all had been told since we headed off to kindergarten for our first day of school." —Jade, age 18

"My school I would say it is a strict school with bullying. They have assemblies about it." —Priyanka, age 15

If the bully were talking to his or her trusted adult, what would the person say? It's likely that you had something to do with the situation, at least in the beginning. It could have been a misunderstanding, unintentional, a joke gone too far, or maybe even something mean you did first. Be honest with yourself about your role in the situation, and include that in your defense. It's possible that a sincere apology or explanation of your role will assist in changing the situation.

Write a script of what you plan to say when you approach the bully about the behavior. Never make assumptions about how the bully is feeling—tell him or her what you see and hear and how it makes you feel. Use statements starting with *I* instead of *you*. Making your bully feel threatened will likely make the situation worse! Once you have some statements written out, practice them with people you trust. Do some role-play, and pretend you're in the situation. It's good to imagine a bad situation and how you would handle it because then, when you're in that situation, you will have already thought about how to proceed. Saying your chosen statement over and over in your head or to friends will make it roll off your tongue when the time is right.

Be wary of allowing someone else to stand up to your bully for you. While your trusted adult may be able to assist in contacting the authorities or your school, you need to be the one making the complaint and fixing the problem. You could get bullied even more if someone else it taking responsibility for the issue.

If you are being bullied for something that really is just part of who you are—such as your appearance, sexuality, intelligence, interests, family, or something else—try to keep a sense of humor about the situation. Singer Justin Bieber, who is frequently harassed online and called a girl, says, "I'm not mad, I'm 16 and I [really] don't have chest hair. You just have to laugh at yourself. It's funny."[10]

If you have truly confronted your bully but nothing has changed, it's time to get extra assistance. You should always do this right away if you feel physically threatened by a bully. If the bullying is happening at school, ask your trusted adult to set up a meeting for both of you with a teacher or school administrator who could help. Make sure that you are present at this meeting; it's about you after all! Calmly and factually explain what has been going on and what you've done to try to fix the problem. You should focus on how to make the bullying end rather than on any kind of punishment the bully may receive. Ask what the school can do to assist in this situation, and ask what to do if the suggested solution does not work in a reasonable amount of time. It is your right to be a member of the school community, and you need to be willing to do your part.

If the bullying is happening outside of school, alert the police. If you are feeling threatened that very moment, call 911. If not, look up your police department's website to get its nonemergency number. With your trusted adult by your side, call and ask how to handle a threatening bullying situation. The police will look at the issue from both sides, so have documentation ready about what you've already done. Documentation includes a list of days and times that the bullying happened, specifics on the behaviors and words used, as well as your attempts to discuss the situation with the bully. Be as specific as possible, and always, always tell the truth, even if it's embarrassing or might get you in trouble too. Do not remove your half of the conversation; even if it shows that you were part of the problem, the fact that you're working on a solution will matter more.

Documentation of cyberbullying shows the online interactions between you and your bully. You can save the messages or texts. If the message is on the computer screen but not savable, you can capture it in a screen shot. In Windows, press the *Print Screen* button, usually found on your keyboard above the arrow keys. On a Mac, the keyboard shortcut is Command-Shift-3. These commands put a picture of the monitor into the computer's memory as if you were copying it. Save the picture by pasting it into a word processing document. Make note of the date and time, the people involved (identifying screen names if needed), and any other contextual information. Save the file, and you have a record of the exchange. You can also print out copies.

What to Do When You Are the Bully

When you realize that you have bullied another person, do you feel remorse? It may be deep inside, in a place that you would never tell anyone else about. Sometimes bullying comes out of peer pressure because your need to be accepted by your friends is stronger than your desire to be nice to a particular person.

If you realize you've been bullying someone, the first thing to do is to stop. Find a way to apologize to your victim. Then find a way to include that person in a social setting to show others that you are being respectful. Ask your friends to be accepting as well.

Warning Signs That Your Friends Are Cyberbullying[11]

- They encourage you to be mean to another person.
- They switch screens or don't let you see what they're doing when you come upon them unexpectedly.
- They get upset if they are restricted from the computer or phone.
- They don't want to talk about what they're doing online.
- They appear to be using many different accounts, especially ones that allow anonymous registration.
- They appear to be using an account belonging to someone else.

It is important to acknowledge your behavior and the outcome, even if it's only to yourself. If you ever feel guilty about something you've done, remember that feeling when interacting with that person again. It can be a subtle shift in your behavior, or it could be as much as turning your friends away from the victim as well. Make a rule for yourself: "I will never attack another person in any way for any reason." Talk about your rule and suggest that your friends do the same. Peer pressure can be used for good as well as evil.

What to Do When Your Friends Are Being Bullied

Witnessing bullying and not saying or doing anything about it gives the bully the idea that you approve of his or her actions even if you do not. If you disapprove of something, speak up. Even a subtle comment or shake of your head can make it clear that you're not okay with what the other person is doing, and that could change his or her behavior. And it is possible to let your friends know how you feel without outright bringing it up. Of course, if you can bring it up and have a private conversation about your feelings, that's the most powerful deterrent of all.

Warning Signs That Your Friends Are Being Cyberbullied[12]

- They appear depressed, angry, or frustrated, especially after using an electronic device.
- They unexpectedly stop using their computer or phone.
- They are nervous or jumpy about e-mails or texts.
- They don't want to talk about what's wrong.
- They are uncomfortable going to school or other public places.
- They are withdrawing from friends or family with no apparent cause.

When you see bullying happening, it is important to do something about it. There is a difference between reporting something to solve the problem and being a snitch, which you do when you want to get someone else in trouble or make yourself look good. Use your avenues to report bad behavior to improve your community.

Sticking up for other teens can also send a message to a bully that you won't tolerate his behavior if he or she aims it at you.

Websites Where Bullying Is the Norm

There are websites that set up situations that encourage bullying. JuicyCampus .com focused on gossip and rants about universities, and other sites have replaced it since it closed in 2009. 4chan.org is a forums site that encourages an "anything goes" attitude, with around a million visits per day. Formspring .me, a website, and Honesty Box, a Facebook application, allow anonymous questions that the user can answer. ChatRoulette.com arranged anonymous video chats that were, at its peak, often R-rated. These sites are practically

What Teens Are Saying

"When I see [online bullying], I try to diffuse the situation or defend the person being bullied, but more often than not, kids are getting sneakier about it so that they don't get caught. Too often, people of power, i.e., principals, parents, teachers, etc., overlook bullying because the bully simply denies the accusation brought against them." —Bow, age 20

"My school claims that it stops bullying, but in reality, I don't think they really care. I see real bullying all the time, and the teachers ignore that and attack the people who are playfully and non-maliciously teasing." —Jack C., age 14

made for bullying due to their anonymous nature and high percentage of teen users.

The owners of these sites maintain that users choose to be there. Dan Peguine, creator of Honesty Box, says, "Honesty Box is safer than sketchy anonymous notes people get in their bags or on their lockers."[13] It is clear that teens who use these sites choose to be there despite any possibilities for bullying.

Formspring administrator Sarahjane Sacchetti says that many anonymous comments that users were responding to had been posted by the user in the first place.[14] Formspring became a place for frustrated teens to stand up for themselves against perceived injustice and unpopularity. By posting self-harassing messages, the teens were able to get attention from friends and family who read their answers. It is common for teens to leap to the rescue of a friend who has responded to such an attack. It also may allow the users to appear cooler than they feel they are, since only the most popular people are hated with such ferocity.

So while there is definitely true bullying going on through these websites, always remember that things may not be as they seem.

ChatRoulette

Do you ever tire of chatting with just people you know? That's how 17-year-old Andrey Ternovskiy, from Moscow, Russia, felt. So he developed a website that allowed people to video chat randomly.

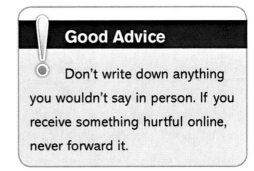

Good Advice

Don't write down anything you wouldn't say in person. If you receive something hurtful online, never forward it.

Ternovskiy explains, "I've always wanted that kind of site. My friends and I used to video chat over Skype quite often, but that got boring after a while. I always knew who was waiting for me and who I would be speaking to."[15] He had found that meeting new people was interesting while working in his uncle's store one summer. When he didn't find what he wanted online, Ternovskiy spent a few days writing code and told people about the site on his favorite forum.

ChatRoulette.com was very popular for just a little while. Launched in November 2009, ChatRoulette quickly grew in both use and popularity, with around 2 million users by March 2010. It was mentioned on talk shows, parodied on *South Park*, and written about in the *New York Times*. But it was starting to fall in popularity by June, and just a few months later, it became a has-been.

The problem was that the mystery and excitement of meeting random people was quickly replaced with the knowledge that it was mostly just men with their pants off. At the height of the website's popularity, 89 percent of the users were male, and users were twice as likely to find a sign requesting female nudity than to actually see it. Even worse, 1 in 8 uses was R-rated or worse. It didn't take long for the users to decide that all they had to do to avoid this kind of bullying was to log off.

Ternovskiy isn't giving up. He has found a way to automatically recognize inappropriate images in ChatRoulette and says that he has gotten the flasher rate down to 1 in 200 by permanently banning the misbehaving users. He is also looking into ideas about how to use his website in new and interesting ways.

What Teens Are Saying: Grace's Formspring Rant

Cyberbullying is so common these days, it's difficult to find a teenager who hasn't experienced it to some degree. I think the worst website for this is Formspring—a "question" site where comments can be anonymously submitted to the user. I had this at one stage, but didn't even consider the amount of abuse I would receive. Soon, after people saw on Facebook that I had it, I was receiving anonymous abuse where people attacked me with petty insults, name calling, degrading comments about my general appearance, [all in] very poor spelling and grammar. At first, this upset me quite a bit, but I responded to everything with rational and cool-headed retorts that the "Formspring Nazi's" couldn't even flaw. Eventually, one comment blended into the other, and it all became quite unoriginal.

This sort of thing tends to happen with "keyboard warriors." I believe teenagers take cyberbullying far too seriously in instances like these. The insignificant people doing this anonymous defamation are obviously not worth listening to. For every hate comment I got, I received more positive comments from my friends to slam it. If you know who you are—and have friends who appreciate you for that—you honestly don't need anyone's bullshit (for want of a better word). I believe in standing strongly for who you are, and if people have to sink so low as to attack you from behind a computer screen—then don't even give it a second thought! These people infuriate me in the way that they are making themselves so blatantly pathetic.

4chan

A teen who called himself *moot* was 15 when he decided to start 4chan in 2003. He and his friends on a forum on Something Awful wanted a place to store images from anime and manga, Japanese cartoons, and comic books. He took the name

What Teens Are Saying

"I think it's interesting to find out what people really think that they don't have the guts to say to you. If it's hurtful, you have to remind yourself that it doesn't really mean anything." —Ariane, quoted in the *New York Times*[16]

"In the past the worst kind of online bullying was Honesty Box on Facebook. I've had people leave messages that were just one word insults, but they still hurt. I've also been accused of sending an honesty box message, that I didn't send, and had the girl and her friends refuse to talk to me at school or believe me when I tried to explain that it wasn't me. I haven't used HB or heard of anyone else using it in awhile, and I don't know if that's because my group of friends has gotten older and grown out of it, or if it's just not used anymore."
—Averill, age 18

from the popular 2chan image forum in Japan, which also focuses on anime and manga.

4chan is famous for its random forum, called /b/, where literally anything goes, including severe bullying. It was within /b/ that many popular Internet *memes*—a culture concept that spreads via the net—have formed, including lolcats, Rockrolling, and Pedobear.

Despite 4chan's rule number 2, "If you are under the age of 18, or it is illegal for you to view the materials contained on this website, discontinue browsing immediately,"[17] teens are flocking to the site. Nineteen percent of the users are aged 13 to 17.

Online Resources for Cyberbullying

- MTV's A Thin Line—www.athinline.org/
- Cyberbullying Research Center—www.cyberbullying.us/

- Cyberbully 411—Cyberbully411.com
- National Council for the Prevention of Crime—www.ncpc.org/cyberbullying
- Pacer Center's Teens against Bullying—www.pacerteensagainstbullying .org/
- Stomp Out Bullying—www.stompoutbullying.org/
- Stop Cyberbullying—www.stopcyberbullying.org

! Justin Bieber's Response to Bullying

Justin Bieber, singer and Disney star, faces cyberbullying every day. He told Ellen DeGeneres, "On my YouTube page, there are so many haters. They just say crazy stuff. . . . People are like, 'Look at him, he puts helium in his voice before he sings.'"[18] Justin recommends helping out when you are a bystander (because you might be the next victim) and to be able to laugh at yourself.

What Adults Are Saying

ChatRoulette "demonstrates that there is still so much more that can be unleashed with video online." Andrey Ternovskiy "has the spotlight and the opportunity to do great things." —Chad Hurley, cofounder and chief executive of YouTube.com, quoted in the *New York Times*[19]

Notes

1. Prevent Cyberbullying and Internet Harassment, "Myths and Facts," 2011, http://cyber bully411.org/myths-and-facts.
2. Andrea Pieters and Christine Krupin, "Youth Online Behavior," June 1, 2010, http://safekids .com/mcafee_harris.pdf.
3. National Crime Prevention Council, "Cyberbullying," n.d., www.ncpc.org/newsroom/ current-campaigns/cyberbullying/.
4. Emily Bazelon, "What Really Happened to Phoebe Prince?" *Slate*, July 20, 2010, www.slate .com/id/2260952/entry/2260953/.

5. Christina A. Samuels, "Bullying May Violate Civil Rights, Duncan Warns Schools," *Education Week*, October 26, 2010, www.edweek.org/ew/articles/2010/10/27/10bully.h30.html.

6. Chelsea Bischof, "Bullying Is Never Acceptable; Sometimes, It Kills," *The Record*, June 9, 2010, www.northjersey.com/news/opinions/95932064_Bullying_is_never_acceptable__sometimes__it_kills.html.

7. That's Not Cool, www.thatsnotcool.com.

8. Ken Paulson, "Sophomoric Speech Is Free Speech, Too," *USA Today*, July 19, 2010, www.usatoday.com/news/opinion/forum/2010-07-20-column20_ST_N.htm?loc=interstitialskip.

9. National Crime Prevention Council, "Stop Cyberbullying before It Starts," n.d., www.ncpc.org/resources/files/pdf/bullying/cyberbullying.pdf.

10. Brad Wete, "Justin Bieber Speaks Out against Bullying on 'Ellen,'" *Entertainment Weekly*, November 3, 2010, http://popwatch.ew.com/2010/11/03/justin-bieber-bullying-ellen-degeneres/.

11. Sameer Hinduja and Justin W. Patchin, "Cyberbullying: Identification, Prevention, and Response," 2010, www.cyberbullying.us/Cyberbullying_Identification_Prevention_Response_Fact_Sheet.pdf.

12. Hinduja and Patchin, "Cyberbullying."

13. Nick O'Neill, "Honesty Box Blamed for Bullying," April 23, 2008, www.allfacebook.com/honesty-box-blamed-for-bullying-2008-04.

14. danah boyd, "Digital Self-Harm and Other Acts of Self-Harassment," *Apophenia*, December 7, 2010, www.zephoria.org/thoughts/archives/2010/12/07/digital-self-harm-and-other-acts-of-self-harassment.html.

15. Yevgeny Kondakov and Benjamin Bidder, "17-Year-Old Chatroulette Founder," March 5, 2010, www.spiegel.de/international/zeitgeist/0,1518,681817,00.html.

16. Tamar Lewin, "Teenage Insults, Scrawled on Web, Not on Walls," *New York Times*, May 5, 2010, www.nytimes.com/2010/05/06/us/06formspring.html.

17. 4chan, "Rules," n.d., www.4chan.org/rules.

18. Wete, "Justin Bieber."

19. Brad Stone, "At YouTube, Adolescence Begins at 5," *New York Times*, May 17, 2010, http://www.nytimes.com/2010/05/17/technology/17youtube.html?_r=3&hpw.

IF YOU'RE FRIENDLY AND YOU KNOW IT: KEEPING UP WITH FRIENDS

"For people of our generation, Facebook is the real world." —Jade, age 18

The Official Social Networking Sites

The main reason for using a social networking site is to keep up with the people you already know. The best way to choose which site to join is to find out what your friends are primarily using. The following information is based on Facebook but will be similarly represented in any social networking site.

Every study about teens using the Internet, as well as a simple look around any school computer lab, shows that the major social networking site of choice today is Facebook.com. Facebook brags that there are over 750 million people worldwide with active accounts. That's 1 in every 9 people on the planet! Americans make up 206.2 million of those accounts, which means that 71 percent of online Americans use Facebook. If in doubt, Facebook is the best to start with and the one we'll focus on in this book.

There are many other social networking sites that people like to use. Google+ is a new site that is modeled after Facebook and is expected to provide some competition. MySpace.com, Tagged.com, Hi5.com, MyYearbook.com, Bebo

Consult your friends when you are deciding what social network to join.

.com, and Friendster.com are similar sites, all with millions of members. There are also specialized sites, such as LinkedIn.com (for business networking), Twitter, and Ning. Some sites have more users in certain countries, such as Orkut.com, which is absolutely huge in Brazil and India but not the United States.

It is interesting how different sorts of people gather on different sites. You can often see trends in how the sites are used and what is discussed there. Each of these major sites compiles a top 10 trends of the year list. Table 4.1 (see page 80) presents the topics most discussed and searched for in 2010 on these three major sites. As you can see, Google is used for entertainment topics, Twitter for news items, and Facebook is a mix.

Signing Up and Finding Your Friends

When you register with a new social networking site, it will ask you for details such as your name, e-mail, gender, and birth date. Most sites don't require you to

Choosing the Best Site for You

"I use Facebook, Twitter, Digg and StumbleUpon; they all offer up unique content or give me access to a specific group of friends." —Jack S., age 17

Do your friends suggest multiple sites? Give one a try. Make an account and fiddle around with it. Then think about these questions:

- Does it seem easy to use? Can you figure out how to do basic stuff?
- Does it know about your friends? If it can't find your friends, it's not useful!
- Does it have privacy features that meet your needs?
- Will your parents approve?
- Check out the groups and public pages—do the comments make sense to you? Do you feel comfortable hanging out online with these people? Do they seem to be your own age, or do they make you feel really old or really young?

There is nothing wrong with opening up a couple of social networking accounts or trying out a new one you've heard of. If you find yourself wanting to use it, you've found the right place! If you forget about it for a while, it's best to delete your account.

give them anything more than that, but they'll ask for more details when you set up your profile. You choose what information about yourself to give out and what to make public.

The site that you are registering with really doesn't have any way to know if you're using your real name. Some things to consider in deciding what name to provide:

- Privacy—is it best for you to use a fake name or a nickname? Is it a rule you've discussed with your parents?
- If you use a fake name, will your friends be able to find you? More important, can people you didn't even think of be able to find you, such

Table 4.1. Top 10 Topics on 3 Major Sites

Google	Facebook	Twitter
Chatroulette	HMU (Hit Me Up)	Gulf oil spill
iPad	World Cup	FIFA World Cup
Justin Bieber	Movies	Inception
Nicki Minaj	iPad and iPhone 4	Haiti Earthquake
Friv	Haiti	Vuvuzela
Myxer	Justin Bieber	Apple iPad
Katy Perry	Games on Facebook	Google Android
Twitter	Mineros/Miners	Justin Bieber
Gamezer	Airplanes	Harry Potter and the Deathly Hallows
Facebook	2011	Pulpo Paul

as that first boyfriend or girlfriend from kindergarten or the friend from summer camp?

- Do most of your friends know you by a nickname? Would they even think to search for your real name?
- Is your most common name a shortening of your full name? Would you prefer to use your full name or your short name?
- Will you be embarrassed by the name you chose in a year? Will it still be relevant?
- What if a prospective employer or college admittance person were to find your Facebook? Would the name you chose be a good reflection of who you are?

- Should you include your middle name or an initial? This is a personal preference, but it might be a way to make a common name easier to find.
- Be cautious not to give too much information about yourself in your user name. For instance, using your birth date as a number to separate yourself from all the other people with your name could be a bad idea since your birth date is one of the things that identity thieves look for. If you do want to use your birth date, don't use the year, and mix up the numbers so it's not obvious that it's your birth date.
- If someone were to search for your user name in a search engine, what would they find out about you? Give it a try before locking yourself into a certain user name.

Also consider your chosen username. This is the single word that you can assign that gives you a nice short web address for your profile. So if you use Facebook and you choose the username of "dogluvr27," your direct address would be www .facebook.com/dogluvr27. When choosing your username, keep in mind that you can never, ever change it! Make it something simple to tell and remember and something completely unembarrassing. It's kind of like a tattoo—do you want to live with it for the rest of your life?

Once you've completed the registration, the first thing that it will encourage you to do is to find your friends by putting in your e-mail account's password. It will see what e-mail you used to register, and it will assume that all your contacts are housed there. Warning! If you let it, it will send an e-mail to every single person in your contact list! How embarrassing! Be very careful not to let it go that far. A better method is to find your friends by putting their names in the general search box at the top of your profile. Once you find one friend, you can usually view his or her friends list and immediately notify mutual friends that you are available to be their friend too.

When you request a friending, it gives you a place to write a personal note. If this person will not immediately recognize you—say you go by a nickname, or it's been a while since you talked to them—it's a good idea to explain who you are. You

What Teens Are Saying

"I do spend (or rather, waste) a lot of time on [social networks] when I'm not really motivated to do my homework instead, mostly on Facebook, but I think the positives outweigh the negatives." —Niki, age 15

"I think that [social networking] is a total waste of time. I mean, why do you want to chat with people online when you can get up and go to them?" —Jake, age 13

"I don't like how some people feel the need to be on all the time. How it is their life. Facebook is my favorite, because I only have an account on it and MySpace is not what my friends use." —Annie, age 16

"MySpace is a social networking site where you can talk to and become friends with people from completely different parts of the world if you have common interests. It is easier to do this over MySpace than it is on Facebook due to the way profiles can be decorated to show what appeals to you. [Facebook] is easy to use, a convenient place to organize events with people, a way to share your photos, see what people think of them and talk to people you've seen around but never really spoke to. I like how you can 'like' the groups, which displays to everyone what you find funny, what annoys you, things you like in general or even how it's supporting a cause." —Grace, age 16

can also send a direct message instead of a friend request, if you feel that's more polite for your current relationship.

When someone sends you a request to be his or her friend, it's time for you to decide if you are comfortable being friends with that person. It's okay to say no! The requestor will not be notified that you refused the request. There are plenty of reasons why you might say no: you don't know him or her that well; you don't like him or her that much; you don't trust him or her to not blab what you say

"[Facebook] often turns into somewhat of a popularity contest, and on occasion can be—at least from my own personal experiences—quite demoralizing while remaining strangely addictive." —Jade, age 18

"I do waste a lot of time on Facebook. I'll go online after school, maybe even chat with some friends for an hour or two (wince), then get off and finish some homework, then go back on to see if anything has changed. I use these sites to pass time." —Niki, age 15

"I love social networking sites because they help share information and entertaining ideas. Facebook . . . is easy to use and is a great way to see what's going on in the world." —Adam, age 17

on your page. Maybe it's your mom or sister, and you don't want either seeing what you're doing! Sometimes a person will repeatedly send friend requests; that's when it's best to speak up and let him or her know why you don't want to approve the request. Most people won't even notice you didn't agree.

Most major social media sites will suggest people for you to friend based on the fact that one or more of your friends is also friends with them. Sometimes these suggestions are really good and will connect you with someone you want on your page whom you forgot to add. Other times, the site is just guessing. The rule of thumb here is to think about how you respond to these suggestions and don't friend someone just because one or two of your friends has friended them. It's best if you already know the person in some way.

Creating Your Profile

Filling in your profile is a good next step. You can be very picky about what you provide. There will be a link or tab to your profile, and nearby is an *Edit my profile*

> ## Taking a Good Profile Photo
>
> There is a very common profile photo pose that a lot of people use, where the photo is taken from above, by the subject. Here's how you do it: hold the camera as high as you can in one hand and angle your body so your best side is showing. Tilt your chin down, hold your shoulders back, and look up at the camera with only your eyes. You may need to take a few shots to get a good one, and remember, you can always crop a photo before you upload it to your profile.

link. Check your in-box (also a tab at the top) to see if the website has left you an introductory e-mail about how to get started. It may include links directly to the things you need most.

Start with a good photo of yourself, one that makes you feel good to see. It's best if you're the only person in the photo. Also, make sure that it's a photo people can recognize you in—so the one wearing that creepy Halloween mask is not a good choice. Once your account is established and you've already friended pretty much anyone you would want to, those photos are great, but at first you should make it clear that it's you.

Social networking sites will ask you things like where you live, other ways to contact you (such as your instant messaging log-in or other e-mail), your interests, opinions, school and job information, photos to share, and your favorite videos or bands. You can determine how much of this information is displayed on your profile, as well as limit some of it to friends and some of it to anyone. If it's not clear who will see it in the *Edit profile* page, check for privacy settings.

Some social network sites—most notably, MySpace—allow you to decorate the background of your profile. This is the page that other people will see when they visit you, not the page you will see when you log in. Often, there are themes that you can choose from, or you can create your own. You can choose colors and a background image and rearrange where things show up on the page. As you

Taking a photo from a high angle makes for a more attractive picture.

change things around, it will give you a preview to be sure that it looks good before changing it.

There are also websites that will help you customize your profile page. For up-to-date ideas and themes, search the Internet with the name of the site and the word *customize*. For instance, *customize MySpace* will get you tons of sites that provide free themes, layouts, and backgrounds.

Visiting Your Friends and Staying Up-to-Date

The main point of social networking sites with friends is to keep your friends up-to-date on your life—namely, through *status updates*. These are short updates that you enter on your main page. It will ask things like what you're doing now, what's on your mind, or what you're up to. Your updates should be short and to the point, usually limited to 140 or 160 characters (same as a text message). You can include a link to a website, picture, or video by pasting the website address

What Teens Are Saying

"My main purpose using Facebook (the main one I use) is to stay connected with my friends and family all over the world. Nothing is better than talking to them sharing pictures/moments of our lives even we are not together."
—Priyanka, age 15

"I rarely post on Twitter or MySpace, just because my Facebook is more inclusive of just my friends and private to others." —Niki, age 15

"I enjoy social networking sites, because I find they are a way you can keep in touch with friends and see what's going on with your peers. Sites like Facebook (my personal favorite) are good for this, as everyone is on it these days."
—Grace, age 16

"I go on Facebook because it's interesting to read what some of my friends have to say." —Annie, age 16

"I think [social networks] are an invaluable resource that are rarely used to their potential. They all offer up unique content or give me access to a specific group of friends." —Jack S., age 17

"I think that they are helpful in finding and keeping friends but they cause us problems with our parents and our grades. They also help in communication but hurt it in the same way." —Vicki, age 16

"You get to connect with friends that you don't see that often, you get to talk to girls you wouldn't normally talk to in school because they are popular. What I hate about all social networking sites is that they can eat up your time."
—Daniel, age 17

into the box. When you post a status update, it is displayed on the main pages of all your friends.

So after setting up your own profile with all the things that are important to you, it's time to see what's important to your friends. Your list of friends is usually on the left side of your main navigation screen. Click on the photo or name of a friend to view his or her profile.

The first thing to do when you visit a friend's page is to say hi. You do this by adding a status update to her or his profile. Remember that anyone else who visits or follows your friend can see your note. If you want to send something privately, send it via message instead (through your mail in-box).

Additionally, the updates that your friends have made appear on your main page. If this gets overwhelming, look for a way to control what is displayed on your page. It's usually a very small *x* on the right side of any status update. You can choose to block everything that a certain person says or just posts from an application that you aren't interested in.

The second purpose of social networking sites is to comment on what your friends have displayed. Every status update, photo, video, note, blog, application, or whatever else has a way to comment on it, usually by clicking on the word *comment* somewhere on the item. When writing a comment, remember that everyone else who looks at your friend's page will see your comment too. This is another place where it's best to think about what you say first.

There are also ways to share the posts of your friends. This allows you to repost the item on your profile for your friends to see. You can usually add a comment about it in the process. Do this by clicking the *Share* button, if there is one.

Apps

Social networking sites offer more than just profile pages and status updates. There are thousands of programs called *apps*, short for *applications*, for you to

What Is Twitter?

"Twitter was just a waste of time. No-one really cares about what you're doing every other minute unless you're a celebrity, and that's essentially the only people who use Twitter." —Grace, age 16

"Using [Twitter] seems so obsessive." —Adam, age 17

Twitter is another very popular social networking option but one that is used primarily by adults. Only 8 percent of online teens use Twitter, according to a Pew Internet survey from September 2009.[1] It is simpler than Facebook; all you can do with Twitter is post status updates. Twitter averages 95,000,000 posts, or *tweets*, per day!

Twitter is most useful when you have a group of followers who can work together on a common goal. For instance, a web designer who is part of a professional Twitter network might post a tweet about a problem to get the input of all her followers. Working together, this network can find a solution. This is especially useful for a person who works alone or is the only person doing his job in an office or company. This could also work for a homeschooled student looking for input on an assignment or for a college student depending on friends from high school for support. While this kind of dialogue is possible in other forums, Twitter is real time and allows for friends of friends to get involved too.

A story of the power of Twitter started on April 10, 2008, when American graduate student James Buck and his Egyptian translator, Mohammed Maree,

use as well. When you want to use an app, you have to install it. Instructions for doing that will appear when you click on it. Some apps get very intrusive, so be smart about what you allow access to your information. Check the privacy settings regarding applications to set rules for any app you use.

Finding apps that are worth your time is a personal pursuit. You are most likely to find them by looking at what your friends are using and talking about in were arrested in Egypt for viewing an antigovernment protest. On the way to police station, Buck tweeted one word: "Arrested." "The most important thing on my mind was to let someone know where we were so that there would be some record of it . . . so we couldn't [disappear]," Buck later said.[2] Colleagues in the United States immediately jumped to action, resulting in Buck's college sending a lawyer to represent him. Buck was released in less than 24 hours, and he sent a follow-up tweet saying simply, "Free." It took nearly 3 months for Maree to be released, due in part to Buck's campaign to have him freed—using Twitter.

Twitter Abbreviations

Since each tweet is limited to 140 characters, Twitter users have created a language all their own. Here are some common terms:

tweet: to send a post via Twitter; also, a single post

tweeter: a user who reads and posts tweets

RT (retweet): forwarding a tweet that you received to your own followers; it's considered polite to indicate that it's a retweet and who you got it from

 # (hash tag): used to add a searchable category tag

@username: putting @ in front of a username links to that user's profile

#FF (follow Friday): a way to share your favorite Tweeters with your own followers

OH (overheard): quoting funny or silly things people overhear

their status updates or what they have linked to on their profile. You can also do a search in your favorite search engine for "most popular apps" and the name of the site you are using.

Apps tend to be one of four types: games, quizzes, profile enhancers, and postings.

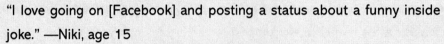

Posting So Only Certain People Understand

"I love going on [Facebook] and posting a status about a funny inside joke." —Niki, age 15

It's called *social steganography* by the people who study such things. The idea is that you say things in such a way that only the people you want to understand will. It could be quoting a movie you know your mom hasn't watched or mentioning a situation without using names that only the friend you confided in (or the person you're mad at) will recognize. The message is meaningless to the majority of your network but meaningful to those who matter. It's a way to be private when everything you say is out in the open.

Researcher danah boyd explains, "Social steganography is one of the most common techniques that teens employ. They do this because they care about privacy, they care about misinterpretation, they care about segmented communication strategies." She goes on to liken the current use of steganography on social networking sites with the use of hidden messages in spy movies or how parents spell out words when young children shouldn't know what they're talking about. She concludes, "I'd expect that [teens are] learning more nuanced ways of managing privacy than any of us adults. Why? Because they have to. The more they live in public, the more I expect them to hide in plain sight."[3]

Games

You can play anything from poker to simple point-and-click games on social networking sites. Many depend on having friends playing the game too or at least willing to install the app even if they never use it. See chapter 13 for more information about games.

Finding New Friends Online

Some places to look for new friends:

Discussion groups: find those websites that have forums to discuss things you are interested in. Getting involved in the conversations will introduce you to all sorts of new people.

Chat rooms: again, find chat rooms that are discussing topics that interest you.

Dating social networks: some social networking sites include a dating component. Look for one that caters to teens.

Regular social networks: sometimes the best way to find a new friend is through an old one. Check out the profiles of the friends of your friends and talk to your friend for an introduction.

Quizzes and Trivia

It seems that there is a quiz on literally everything, from favorite color to totem animals to uncomfortable sexual positions. Some of them are fun and well done, but most are just silly. There are apps that allow you to write your own quizzes, which is why sometimes you see quizzes that are very badly done. You can also find trivia apps on just about every TV show, movie, or band. Again, these will vary in quality, as some are created by users.

While it can be fun to compare your results with friends, keep in mind that these apps are looking at a variety of personal information on your profile. If you choose to do a quiz, it's a good idea to delete the app once you're done.

Profile Enhancers

Your friends' profiles may include information that was provided by apps. These

Help, It's Too Much!

Do you find yourself spending so much time keeping up with your friends online that your homework suffers? What do you do when you have so many social networking log-ins that you can't keep track? Get a dashboard!

Social media dashboards are websites that allow you to have all your social media sites combined on one page for easy viewing. You don't get to see everything from each site, but you can adjust the settings to show what's important to you.

There are lots of dashboards to choose from. Major sites, such as Google and Yahoo, offer a customizable homepage on which you place widgets or gadgets that access your other sites. You can also find out what sites offer this product by searching online for "social media dashboard." Be aware that you are giving your password to a third party when you use a dashboard. Choose one that you can trust.

may be information such as relatives or places they've been. While these apps can be very useful in providing information for your friends, keep in mind that the app company can access all this information.

Dating social networking sites also usually have a matchmaking feature of some sort, letting you see information from other members' profiles and marking whether or not you are interested in them. Before participating in these features, consider whether you are comfortable with strangers rating you solely on your current profile picture.

Postings

Some apps will post to your profile on a regular basis. It may be a daily inspirational quote or cute photo. They may provide reminders such as friends' birthdays or events you've agreed to attend. Or they may be gift apps that allow you to send virtual items to your participating friends. The best use of a posting app is to set up another site that you use often to post on your social networking profile. For instance, you can tell Facebook to post a status update for every video you favorite on YouTube. Remember that you can remove these apps when the posts are no longer of interest to you.

When you're no longer using an app, it's a good idea to uninstall it. It will still have the private information you gave it permission to use even when it no longer needs it. Under the settings or account tab, there should be a section just for applications where you can remove apps. Alternatively, you may find that a friend is playing an app that posts a lot of status updates that are not of interest to you. You can block all notices from a certain app by clicking on the *x* on the right-hand side of each status update. You can block certain apps without blocking other things that the friend is saying.

Communicating Online

The online world has a language and culture all its own. There are rules about how to speak and what is expected, which you need to learn to be comfortable there. You speak *netspeak*, express emotions with *emoticons*, and follow the rules of *netiquette*. All these terms are netspeak themselves, usually an abbreviation of a phrase. For instance, *emoticon* is a mash-up of *emotion* and *icon*, meaning a picture that expresses how you feel. Netspeak and netiquette use the common shortening of *network* combined with *speaking* and *etiquette*. The following is basic information about these concepts to get you started.

Figuring out netspeak can be a challenge. This is a list of commonly used netspeak, but if what you're looking for isn't here, direct your favorite search engine to *netspeak* or even the term you're trying to look up. Sometimes it's possible to figure out a netspeak word by saying it out loud as it looks.

143 = I love you

404 = clueless

4eva = forever

911 = emergency

addy = website address

afk = away from keyboard

ama = ask me anything

bc or cuz or cos = because

bf = boyfriend

bff or bestie = best friend

bi or bai = bye

boi = boy

bs = bullshit

btw = by the way

CD9 or Code 9 = parents are around

cex = sex

convo = conversation

def = definitely

dftba = don't forget to be awesome

dif or diff = difference

f@ = fat

fam = family

fb = Facebook

g = grin

gf = girlfriend

grrl = girl

gtg = got to go

hai = hi

i8y = I hate you

icymi = in case you missed it

idk = I don't know

IM = instant messaging

imo or imho = in my (humble) opinion

interwebz = Internet

irl = in real life

j/k or jk = just kidding

k or kk = okay

kthxbai = Okay, thanks, bye!

less than three (<3) = love (a heart is a "less than" symbol and the numeral 3)

lol or lawl = laughing out loud

mwah = a kiss

n/a/s/l = name, age, sex, location

nmu = Not much, you?

nsfw = not safe for work, meaning that it's only safe to watch in private

p/w or pwd = password

pics or pix = pictures

prolly = probably

pron = porn

rawr = expression of affection, because it's how dinosaurs say "I love you"

rly = really

rofl = rolling on the floor laughing

roflmao = rolling on the floor laughing my ass off

s = smile

skool or skl = school

srsly = seriously

thx or ty = thank you

tmi = too much information

ttyl = talk to you later

w/e or whatev = whatever

warez = pirated software

wtf = what the f**k?

zomg = oh my god with extra emphasis

Netspeak is also written using letters or symbols to replace sounds. Here are some common uses:

& = "and" sound, like b& = banned

@ = letter a

0 = letter o

2 = "to" sound, like 2gether = together

2 = to or too

3 = letter e

4 = "for" sound, like b4 = before

4 = letter a

8 = "-ate" sound, like b8 = bait

c = "see" sound

r = are or our

u = you

z = "s" sound, like gamez = games

There is also *1337 speak*, where digits and special symbols replace letters in common words. "1337" represents the letters *leet*, short for *elite*. It is intended to be writing that only knowledgeable users will understand, therefore making it accessible only to the elite. For example, the main character of *Little Brother*, by Cory Doctorow, uses the handle of Winston, spelled "W1n5t0n." There is a funny scene in the book where the principal of Winston's school says the name is "W one N five T zero N," showing that he does not understand leet speak.

Translate leet speak by sounding out the words based on appearance. With some practice, you can learn to see the symbols as words. If in doubt, search on the Internet for *leet speak dictionary*.

The term *emoticon* is a combination of *emotion* and *icon*. Emoticons use symbols and letters to create pictures that indicate a mood or physical response. These are powerful because they allow you to express nonverbal indicators in your text communication. However, emoticons are not considered professional and should

What Teens Are Saying

"I like using emoticons. They are a half-decent way to display emotions in a situation where they can't be seen." —Annie, age 16

" =] :) =[:(:D<3 " —Averill, age 18

" :(:) ;) " — Priyanka, age 15

"I use: :) :(and XD frequently." —Ava, age 16

"I use smiley faces all the time in texts and online, as I'm sure you've noticed. :)" —Niki, age 15

"I regularly use all emoticons and netspeaks. There are very few teenagers do not use." —Adam, age 17

not be used in formal communication, such as homework assignments or college essays. They are best used in chat, IM, e-mail, or status updates.

You read an emoticon by seeing the picture in the letters. This is a skill that some people struggle to learn, but given practice, you will start to see emoticons without even realizing they are symbols. For instance, a colon and parenthesis make a simple smiling face if you look at it sideways from the left. :) The colon represents the eyes; the parenthesis the mouth.

Here are some common emoticons:

Smiles: :) :-) (: =) => :> =^_^=

Very big smile: :D

Wink: ;) ;-)

Sad: :( ):

Shock: 8I

Cool: 8)

Confused: %)

Crying: :') :~)

Angry: >:(

Sticking out your tongue: :P :)~

Surprised: :O

Scared: =><=

Fail: :&

Undecided: :/ ^_^

Evil: >:)

Angel: 0:)

Heart: <3

Hug: { }, often with the person's name inside, the number of brackets indicating the size of the hug: {{{Aiden}}}

Rose: @--->---

You can also use special symbols to create emoticons. If you are using a word processing program, there is likely a symbol chart to use under "Font" or "Insert." Online you need to know the Alt code to create the symbols. You can find the complete chart by searching for "Alt codes" in your favorite search engine. Use them by holding down the Alt key while typing the number, and the symbol will appear.

Rock on: ¥ ^_^ ¥ Alt-0165 for the Latin Y

Heart: ♥ Alt-3

Music Notes: ♪ Alt-13 or ♫ Alt-14

Divided by sign: √ Alt-251

Netiquette is a combination of the words *etiquette* and *network*, meaning your online manners. The point is that you treat people online the same way that you would treat them in person or over the telephone, with politeness and respect. Never forget that you are talking to a person even if it feels like you just send letters off into space.

General manners:

- Be polite and courteous. Before hitting *Send*, think, "Would I say this face-to-face?"
- Send well-written and brief e-mails that are not full of spelling mistakes or bad grammar.
- Proofread everything you send!
- Don't interrupt or monopolize conversations in chat or IM.
- Don't spam your friends with requests for money or personal assistance.
- Be forgiving of other people's mistakes, but politely and privately tell them if they keep making the same mistake.
- Do not insult someone else personally. If you are insulted, walk away from the computer, and do not respond for at least 24 hours, if at all. Remember that it may have been a misunderstanding.
- Respect the privacy of the other people while protecting your own.

Specific online manners:

- Say goodbye when you leave a chat or IM conversation.
- Avoid writing in all caps, unless you really are yelling.
- Avoid sarcasm, as it does not come across as sarcasm in text.
- Avoid cussing, gross, or coarse language unless you would use it with that person in real life.
- Put asterisks around a word to give it *emphasis.*

About forwarding e-mails:

- Never forward something you didn't read yourself.
- Research before forwarding, especially e-mails that are alarming. Doing an Internet search for keywords in the e-mail will likely give you more information about the message. Try www.snopes.com as well.
- Don't send an attachment to people who don't need it.
- Respect a request to not send forwards.

Social Networks Created by Teens

Facebook.com

While attending Harvard, Mark Zuckerberg created a social networking site allowing other Harvard students to rate their classmates. This involved hacking into student directories, and Zuckerberg was nearly expelled over the website, but it generated over 450 visits in the first 4 hours! Zuckerberg used the idea for an art history assignment, comparing historical people instead, which was also opened to his classmates. Zuckerberg saw that there was an interest in this kind of communication, so he created Facebook, which was launched in 2004. Originally, membership was limited to just Harvard students, and more than half the students joined within the first month. Within 2 years, interest was so great that the site was opened to anyone who wanted to join. The site reached 500 million members after just 6 years and is estimated to be worth over $20 billion. Ninety percent of teens with a social networking account use Facebook, according to a survey published in October 2010.

You can learn more about the details of Mark Zuckerberg's invention in the book *The Accidental Billionaires: The Founding of Facebook—A Tale of Sex, Money, Genius, and Betrayal*, by Ben Mezrich, or in the movie based on the book, *The Social Network*. Be aware, though, that Zuckerberg has spoken out about this story, saying that it's not an accurate portrayal of how things really happened. In an interview with *Business Insider*, Zuckerberg said that moviemakers don't understand that "someone might build something because they like building things"[4] rather than getting revenge on a girl who dumped him.

Whateverlife.com

Whateverlife.com started as a hobby coding HTML that has turned into a social network for teens that has made its creator, Ashley Qualls, into a millionaire—

all from ads on the site. Ashley started the project when she was 14 as a way to share MySpace profiles and other HTML coding with her friends. Everything on the site is free because advertisements more than pay for the site. It attracts hundreds of thousands of visitors daily, mostly teen girls, and Ashley has turned down numerous lucrative offers to sell the website from major players, including MySpace. Ashley said, "No matter what your age is, never limit yourself!"[5]

One of the best features on the website is the tutorials, written for teens by teens. You can find assistance for all things social networking, from setting up accounts to decorating profiles to writing your own HTML.

MyYearbook.com

Siblings David and Catherine Cook, both in high school, created myYearbook.com in 2005, originally intended just for their own New Jersey school. Catherine posts, "Dave and I started myYearbook with only one thing in mind—making meeting new people as fun and easy as possible!"[6] In April 2010, the site announced that it had reached 1 million posts per day on the myYearbook Chatter stream.

The fun thing about myYearbook is all the games and social interactions. The site encourages you to meet new people through games such as Match, where you rate other users' photos; Ask Me, where you post and answer questions; and Owned! where you use in-game money to purchase other users as virtual pets.

Notes

1. Amanda Lenhart et al., "Social Media and Young Adults," February 3, 2010, www.pewInternet .org/Reports/2010/Social-Media-and-Young-Adults/Part-3/4–Twitter-among-teens-and-adults.aspx?r=1.
2. Mallory Simon, "Student 'Twitters' His Way out of Egyptian Jail," April 25, 2008, www.cnn .com/2008/TECH/04/25/twitter.buck/index.html.
3. danah boyd, "Social Steganography: Learning to Hide in Plain Sight," *DML Central*, August 23, 2010, www.zephoria.org/thoughts/archives/2010/08/23/social-steganography-learning-to-hide-in-plain-sight.html.
4. Anthony Ha, "Mark Zuckerberg: Facebook Doesn't Make Real Profits, and That's Okay," *So-

cial Beat, October 16, 2010, http://venturebeat.com/2010/10/16/facebook-mark-zuckerberg-profits/.

5. "About Us," 2011, www.whateverlife.com/about_us.php.

6. "Our Story," 2011, www.myyearbook.com/our_story.php.

OTHER WAYS TO SOCIALIZE WITH FRIENDS ONLINE

"I think [social media sites are] useful because we are in contact with friends and family." —*Thomas, age 13*

Specialized Social Media Sites

Websites such as Ning.com and Wikia.com allow users to create specialized social networks. That means that you can create a wiki that is all about your favorite movie, adding content such as information about the actors, photos from the set, and any other tidbits you have. Then your friends (and strangers) can join and add their own content or start discussions. These sites function much as Facebook does, but they allow you to guide the specialized content yourself.

Wikis

A *wiki* is a website that allows users to create and edit pages on the site. The most well-known wiki is Wikipedia.org. Launched in 2001, Wikipedia is a free online encyclopedia that anyone can edit. All changes are logged and watched by other users, so although misinformation shows up on Wikipedia, it is often found and fixed very quickly. *Nature* magazine compared Wikipedia to *Encyclopaedia Britannica* and found an equivalent amount of errors between

> ### Some Stats about Wikipedia[1]
>
> - 18,900,000 articles on Wikipedia as of May 2011, with about 9,000 added daily.
> - 11,600,000 edits made on Wikipedia articles per day in May 2011.
> - 62 percent of Internet users under the age of 30 use Wikipedia.[2]

them. The biggest difference, *Nature* reported, was that Wikipedia was in need of a good editor.[3]

Wikipedia is successful because of the 91,000 editors and their expertise and interest in certain topics. These are the people who monitor and edit the contributions of more than 14 million registered users. They also lead behind-the-scene discussions about each page, where interested contributors can decide the best way to convey the information. You can see (and join) these conversations by clicking on the *Discussion* tab at the top of any Wikipedia page.

Use your favorite search engine to find social networks on your favorite topics. Using keywords to describe your topic and adding the word *wiki* will bring up various options. (If Wikipedia takes over your search, add -*Wikipedia* to the search. Adding a dash in front of a term will tell the search engine to remove that term from the search.) Look for website addresses that have the word *wiki* in the domain name, since those sites are likely make-your-own wiki sources. Take some time to look over the site before joining so you don't end up with a low-quality resource.

Ning

Ning.com is a make-your-own social networking site. Ning charges a monthly fee to host a site, but you can join sites for free. Go to Ning.com and put your keywords into the search box at the top of the screen, or you can browse popular sites on the main page. You only need one registration with Ning to join many communities.

What Teens Are Saying

"I use Wikipedia to look up politicians and facts on different things in life. I trust Wikipedia most of the time, because a lot of the things I look up are not of importance and Wikipedia is actually a good reference because most people do not just change things for the fun of it." —Adam, age 17

"I think that sometimes [Wikipedia] is good that users can edit content but I think that a lot of information turns out to be biased in the end." —Daniel, age 17

"I use Wikipedia for school but I think you have to have an account to edit it, so at least they have some protection against false editing." —Jack C., age 14

Unlike wikis, Ning's format follows the general social networks such as Facebook, having profiles, friend lists, status updates, photos, and blogging. The only real difference is that Ning also allows forum discussions for all members.

One popular Ning is http://nerdfighters.ning.com, home of the Nerdfighters. Popular teen fiction author John Green and his musician brother Hank Green decided in 2007 to communicate only via video blogs for an entire year. They grew such a following that a community called Nerdfighteria grew out of their blogs and spread into various websites, forums, and video channels—and a Ning. The community focuses on "decreasing world suck" and spreading the idea that being a nerd is cool.

Blogs and Personal Journals

Another way to keep up with your friends is to keep an eye on their personal websites. Most often, a personal website is a blog or personal journal. These are websites that you can customize and then post your own writing. *Blog* is short for

What Teens Are Saying

"I don't really use a blog as a means of social networking; I more use it as a sort of outlet. I don't really care how many people read it or how many subscribers I have, the point of my blog is for me to attempt to express my thoughts in words. You see, I am a visual thinker; I do not actually think in words. I have to translate what I am seeing/feeling into sentences. So my blog is something I started as a sort of exercise for myself in this matter, and I really do absolutely love it. It gives me a sense of accomplishment and pride when I can look back at what I have written and feel that it says everything I wanted and meant for it to say." —Jade, age 18

"Blogs are a great way to write online for a large audience or even a small audience. I think that blogs are good, but you have to be careful because some people make them just for the ads. I think that blogging is dying because now we have Facebook and such." —Daniel, age 17

"To really use a blog I feel that it must be set up in a completely connected system. The whole Internet is about simplicity, I shouldn't have to use 2 sites to check a blog." —Jack S., age 17

"I rarely if ever use blogs. I think they are boring and kinda useless." —Jack C., age 14

"Status updates are as close as I've come to blogging. :) " —Niki, age 15

"I do write a blog on Xanga. I think it's okay as long as you don't use your real name or information. I blog about the stuff I know no one wants to hear me go on about (again). Status updates are short, so I think blogs are going to stick around. My preference depends on what I want to post." —Ava, age 16

Share your personal thoughts on your blog.

web log, an early Internet term, and it refers to any kind of personal journaling on a website. Anyone can publish a blog, and there are blogs on every topic that you can imagine. If you can't find a blog on the topic you want, you can write your own!

There is a growing movement that says that blogging is a dying art. A Pew Internet study done in September 2009 found that only 14 percent of teens are blogging, down from 28 percent in 2007. It seems that the status updates available on Twitter and other social networking sites are preferred by teens. Status updates are sometimes called *microblogging* because they are very short blogs.

Some people think that texting and 140-character status updates are teaching the younger generations bad writing skills. They claim that teenagers only use textspeak and are losing their ability to compose longer prose, write in complete sentences, follow proper grammar, and spell even common words. Blogging is one way of combating these concerns because it uses all those functions plus the skill of writing for an intended audience.

All the major social networking sites include a blog, notes, or journal option, and you can start by putting up posts there. The benefit of this is that your friends will get notified that you've posted something new. The downside is that these blogs are not nearly as customizable or flexible as the true blog sites, such as Blogger .com, WordPress.com, and LiveJournal.com. All these sites allow you to create a registration, create a blog, and put up your content whenever you want. You can customize the appearance of your blog using provided themes or color schemes or, if you are feeing savvy, creating your own theme. You can also post things that your readers will see every time they visit your site, such as links to your favorite sites, archives of your posts, or even advertisements from your sponsors.

Always keep in mind that a blog is a public website, and unless you change your privacy settings, anyone on the Internet can see what you've posted. This is another place where you need to be aware of what you're posting about yourself. It's even more public than Facebook or MySpace because blog sites do not require readers to have a log-in.

Finding Your Friends' Blogs and How to Follow Them

When you're looking to follow your friend's blog, the best way to find it is to ask where it is. The point of a blog is to share your posts so that any blogger will be happy to give you the address. If that isn't possible for some reason, try a search of the person's name or the name of the blog (if you know it) in your favorite search engine.

There are two ways to keep track of a blog that you want to read. The first is to go to that blog's website on a regular basis. While this gives you a full picture of the site, including how it has been decorated, it can be quite tedious unless the author posts on a regular schedule. It also can be something you forget to do.

The second way to keep track of a blog is through a blog reader. Blogs have a built-in feature called *Really Simple Syndication*, or *RSS*. When you see this orange symbol on a website, that page has an RSS feed that you can subscribe to, so you are notified when there is a change. Blogs use RSS to notify you that a new post has been published.

Feed readers are websites that allow you to subscribe to and read the blogs of your choice. Two major free feed readers are Google Reader (http://google.com/reader) and FeedDemon.com. Google Reader is a part of your Google log-in or Gmail account. FeedDemon is a program that you have to download and install, but it works directly with your Internet browser for easy access. Again, this is a time to ask your friends what they prefer to use.

Once you have set up your feed reader, you visit just that website or program instead of going to each blog website one at a time. It will display any updates since the last time you visited. When you read a blog or click through to the actual website, it marks that entry as read.

The feed reader will give you a place to add new subscriptions. Find the blog you want to follow, and copy its address into that box. The reader will automatically subscribe you to the blog and set up the reader to display recent entries. You can click on the title of the blog entry to go to the website, which is sometimes necessary if the entire blog doesn't display in your feed reader. How much of the blog that displays is set by the owner of the blog.

There is an amazing number of fantastic blogs out there. The basic way to find them is to watch for that orange symbol to show up on a website as you're surfing around in the sites you already use. You can do an Internet search using the keyword *blog* along with whatever topic you would like to read about. Also, there are search engines just for searching blog content. The biggest one is Technorati .com, which indexes more than a million blogs, or you can find a list of blog search engines at Wikipedia.org by searching for *list of search engines* and choosing blog from the content/topic list. Your feed reader likely has ways to search by keyword as well. And, as always, ask your friends what they enjoy!

What Is Tumblr?

"My latest obsession is Tumblr! It's like a Narnia-type world; looks boring and simple from the outside, but as soon as you log in—there's a whole 'nother world! It's so addictive, I all too often find myself just scrolling down my dashboard on Tumblr, finding things that other people have reblogged that appeal to me, reblogging, then continuing to scroll. Hahaha, it's such a sad life . . . " —Grace, age 16

Tumblr is a different sort of blog that easily allows you to share anything and everything you come across. Think of it as a scrapbook for your online life where you can post anything you want to remember. All you do is give it the information or the source; it makes it look right on the page.

You can post anything in any format (text, videos, photos, music, links) from any access point (Internet, e-mail, phone, even voice). You can also customize your page however you like. It allows you to repost things you found to share them with the world. Your friends can follow your tumblr, and you can follow someone's posts in your blog reader.

Some people say that Tumblr is the next big thing. It has combined the best parts of Facebook, MySpace, and Twitter in an easy-to-use, very personal way. Use of the site is growing quickly, with over 20 million blogs as of June 2011. Most important, Tumblr has an 85 percent retention rate, meaning that nearly all of the people who sign up continue using the site. Other social media sites typically have about 50 to 60 percent retention rate. Users are sticking with it, so it must be worth using. Studies are finding that Tumblr is often a teen's second-favorite social media site, after Facebook. Also, Quantcast shows a very high percentage of teens using the site, so you're likely to find your friends there.

What Teens Are Saying

"I love instant messaging! Such a clever invention." —Grace, age 16

"I will talk to people via the Google Chat or Facebook Chat. Those are nice because they're very fast, and convenient." —Annie, age 16

"Facebook is the most convenient for chatting, because your friends are already there, you don't have to ask for and remember a special username to add them specifically, and if they aren't online and you want to tell them something you can just write on their wall." —Averill, age 18

"I love chatting online to my friends; I mostly do this on Facebook."
—Daniel, age 17

"I use Facebook chat to talk to my friends quite often, but I've never instant messaged a person I didn't know personally. I agree that it can be unsafe if people aren't smart about who they talk to." —Niki, age 15

"Facebook and texting usually have the same conversations and purpose, but Omegle is a lot of fun, chatting with strangers, but as soon as you're done with the conversation you can disconnect." —Jack S., age 17

Instant Messaging and Chat Rooms

Another way to keep up with your friends online is by using chat. There are many ways to chat with people online, and some of them are safer and easier than others.

Most social networking sites have a chat feature built in. There will be a place on your main screen, usually at the bottom right of the screen, which lists your friends who are currently online. If you click on the friend's name, it will pop up a chat box that just the two of you can see. It is possible to have multiple chat boxes open at once.

Safety in a Chat Room

When going out into public chat rooms, it's important to keep your safety and privacy at the forefront of your thoughts. Most social networking sites allow you to limit who can see your information and posts, but in a public chat room, it could be literally anyone on the other end. Some people don't behave very well in chat rooms, so keep in mind that you can always log out if you are uncomfortable. Never give out personal information, and be aware of what you are giving out. Sometimes lots of general information can give someone enough clues to track you down.

Instant Messaging Programs

Another way to chat in private is through instant messaging, or IM, although it usually requires registration and often a program to download and install. Once you have it all set up, you click on your friend's name, and it opens a chat box for both of you to use. Some IM programs also have ways to play games or decorate the chat box together.

The most popular instant messaging sites are Yahoo Instant Messenger, AOL Instant Messenger, ICQ, and Windows Live. This is a time when it really matters what your friends are using because you can usually only chat with people who use the same program.

To get started with IM, choose your program and go to the website. There will be a link to download and install the program. It will guide you through creating a log-in and finding your friends who also use that program. To send a message, click on the friend's name in your list.

Some people use IM to send spam. It's a good idea to check the privacy settings of the program. You should be able to turn off the ability for someone not in your friends list to send you a message. And, as always, be smart about who you agree to be friends with.

There are a few IM programs that allow you to access a variety of IM programs at once. An example is Meebo.com, which has the added benefit of being a website rather than a program you have to download. You can access it from any Internet computer and set it up to access your other IM programs. Be aware that you are giving your password to Meebo. It does encrypt it as it sends it out across the Internet, but it is secured in Meebo's database. If this makes you uncomfortable, Meebo may not be the program for you to use.

Meebo works as any other IM program at first: you go the website and create a log-in. Meebo is an IM program just like any other, and you can use it without having any other IM log-ins. If you have a log-in to any of the programs that Meebo partners with, you can sign on via Meebo and have all of your IM registrations available at once. Its list of programs is quite extensive and constantly growing.

Finding Public Chat Rooms

Most social networking sites and IM programs have a way to join public chat rooms. Some of them, such as Meebo, also let you create your own chat room and invite specific friends to join you there. Be sure to use a password so that no strangers can join too. This is a good solution when you have more than one friend whom you want to chat with at a time.

When you access a public chat area, it will give you a list of chat rooms for you to join. Often they are organized by topics so that people can choose to discuss something they are interested in. It's not uncommon for discussions to move to other topics though.

When you choose a room, a chat window will load. It will have a large area for you to see the conversation and a box for you to type your posts, along with a *Send* or *Submit* button to push when you're ready to send. It will also list the other users

---

What Teens Are Saying

"Skype is excellent for non-text based conversation. I rarely use Skype as an IM platform, but recently I've used the video chat a lot, and I'm really glad that I will have that next year when I'm at college, so I can still 'see' my old friends and parents." —Averill, age 18

"Since I have friends all over the world . . . calling them is expensive but an application like Skype is very helpful. You can see them and talk." —Priyanka, age 15

---

in the room, and it usually gives a button to send a private message. Chat programs also have a block or ignore button that you can use to turn off the posts of a single user. This is useful if you are enjoying the conversation but find one person to be rude or annoying.

Voice Chat

There are also ways to speak through the computer, using a microphone or video recorder. Skype is the most popular of the voice/video chat programs. It works just like the other IM programs, including a way to chat via text, plus the ability to "call" the person and speak aloud.

Voice chatting is an alternative to long-distance phone calls, especially when the two parties are in different countries. Anyone with Internet access and some sort of video or microphone can use it to make a free call. Many people also use it to converse while playing video games together. As always, the best one for you is the one that all your friends are already using. Also, all the same privacy and safety rules apply.

What Teens Are Saying

"I think e-mail is a great resource. You can contact others for business and also share ideas. I use gmail, hotmail, and facebook to send messages."
—Adam, age 17

"I use [e-mail] to communicate with friends and teachers." —Annie, age 16

"I prefer e-mail, because you may not get a reply for a couple of days, and so you won't run out of things to say like what happens when you text a person constantly, but also, sometimes, it's not preferable to have to wait for a reply and can be very slow." —Annie, age 16

"I always check my e-mail, like every time when I have spare time on the computer." —Daniel, age 17

"I use gmail and I think it's way better than Facebook. You can do way more on gmail than on Facebook. It's like Facebook and regular e-mail had a love child named gmail." —Jack C., age 14

"E-mail has become more professional than personal these days. I only use to stay connected with the school's network, and something that cannot be done on Facebook." —Priyanka, age 15

"I prefer gmail because it has an IM option that I like to use when my friends are on." —Annie, age 16

"I mainly use e-mail for official use, such as work or school." —Bow, age 20

"I like hotmail because this is how I text people, because I don't have a cell phone I can text people via e-mail." —Daniel, age 17

E-mail

In June 2010, Sheryl Sandberg, chief operating officer of Facebook, told a conference of marketers that "E-mail . . . is probably going away." She stated that only 11 percent of teens use e-mail daily.[4] This has created the belief that teens are no longer depending on e-mail the way that adults do, but other studies disagree.

The Radicati Group released a study on e-mail use in April 2010, explaining that "the number of worldwide e-mail accounts is projected to increase from 2.9 billion in 2010, to over 3.8 billion by 2014."[5] It went on to say that social media is the fastest-growing technology and that IM is growing as well. Meanwhile, the *New York Times* reported that "Internet users collectively sent 107 trillion (yes, that's with a 't') messages in 2010."[6] Obviously this isn't a passing fad.

What about for teens using e-mail though? Another marketing group, Trendline Interactive, did a study in early 2010 asking teens about their social media use. It found that an equivalent numbers of teens used Facebook and e-mail daily, 35 percent and 36 percent, respectively. It also noted that people use the most appropriate tool to get their message across. CEO Morgan Stewart said, "Before sending a message, we consider what channel our target is most likely to respond to."[7]

The simple fact is that teens use what works for their friends and within their community. Niki, age 15, said, "I used to use e-mail a lot, to keep in touch with friends and family, mostly just sending cute pictures or short messages. But now as a teenager, after getting a Facebook profile and a cell phone, I don't really use e-mail as much, and only check it about once a week. Now, instead of using it to communicate with friends and family, I use it primarily to stay informed from groups that I'm involved in or getting coupons and sale notifications from a few of my favorite stores. And even though I'm only a sophomore, I'm being bombarded by e-mails from colleges as well. So, my gmail is mostly used for information rather than communication anymore. Facebook is much more convenient to use for keeping in touch, I think."

What Teens Are Saying

"E-mail will never die as you need it to register on sites and you get notifications with e-mails." —Daniel, age 17

"I do not think that e-mail is dying. I think that the social aspect is, but from a professional side, e-mail is thriving. Most teens now use Facebook to message friends because you can do other things while on there as well, but for school projects, e-mail is strong." —Adam, age 17

"E-mail has a very distinct use, and I don't think that it is dying at all. Facebook is great for messaging friends, but there are plenty of times when I want to get in contact with someone, and they aren't just some Facebook friends. I e-mail customer services, my employer, my parents, colleges, and other people that I have a more formal relationship with all the time, and I don't want those lines of communication to move to Facebook. I also was recently in China, and Facebook is blocked there, so all of my online communication was over e-mail, and it was a great way to stay in touch with people." —Averill, age 18

"In a way, I would say that Facebook and texting are replacing the traditional form of e-mail but e-mail will evolve into a necessary evil if only for the needs of business and spam advertisements." —Jack S., age 17

"I do still use Facebook messaging too—and in I way I suppose it is replacing e-mail. Facebook will only interact with people on Facebook, will not receive messages from anything other than another person on Facebook, and is also a lot less personal than an e-mail address. I prefer Facebook for interacting with friends, but e-mail is *always* useful to have for everything else." —Grace, age 16

"E-mail is a good thing, it's easier than letters or phone calls. I think e-mail will stick around. After all, who wants their boss to see some of those scandalous FaceSpace pictures?" —Ava, age 16

Notes

1. Erik Zachte, "Wikpedia Stats," August 31, 2011, http://stats.wikimedia.org/EN/TablesWikipediaZZ.htm.
2. Kathryn Zickuhr and Lee Raine, "Wikipedia, Past and Present," January 13, 2011, http://pewInternet.org/Reports/2011/Wikipedia.aspx.
3. "Wikipedia Survives Research Test," December 15, 2005, http://news.bbc.co.uk/2/hi/technology/4530930.stm.
4. Austin Carr, "Facebook COO Sheryl Sandberg Is Embracing the End of E-mail, Here's Why," June 16, 2010, www.fastcompany.com/1660619/facebook-coo-sheryl-sandberg-on-the-end-of-e-mail-branding-in-social-networks.
5. Todd Yamasaki, "The Radicati Group, Inc. Releases 'E-mail Statistics Report, 2010–2014,'" April 19, 2010, www.radicati.com/?p=5290.
6. Nick Bilton, "2010 Online, by the Numbers," *New York Times*, January 14, 2011, http://bits.blogs.nytimes.com/2011/01/14/2010-online-the-numbers/.
7. Morgan Stewart, "3 Things about Social Media That May Shock You," May 13, 2010, www.mediapost.com/publications/?fa=Articles.showArticle&art_aid=128100.

THE MOBILE WORLD

"The computer in your cell phone today is a million times cheaper and a thousand times more powerful and about a hundred thousand times smaller [than the one computer at MIT in 1965] . . . so what used to fit in a building now fits in your pocket."
—*Ray Kurzweil[1]*
"I don't think you should be lonely at any time so your phone is company."
—*Priyanka, age 15*

Your phone is really a pocket computer. It has more functions, better connections, and faster processing than the much larger computers you used 5 years ago. The convenience of carrying a computer in your pocket, added to this computing power, makes smartphones and tablet computers the wave of the future—already happening! As of this writing, smartphones and tablet computers haven't yet overtaken computer sales, but it will likely have happened before this book is published in 2012.

PC Magazine's definition of the smartphone is "a cellular telephone with built-in applications and Internet access. Smartphones provide digital voice service as well as text messaging, e-mail, Web browsing, still and video cameras, MP3 player and video viewing. In addition to their built-in functions, smartphones can run myriad applications, turning the once single-minded cellphone into a mobile computer."[2]

The future of the Internet is mobile access, which means that there are more ways to access the Internet through your smartphone every day. However, if it seems like everyone has a smartphone, you'd be wrong! One 2010 study found that 67 percent of 15- to 24-year-olds had a mobile phone but only 28 percent were

A computer in every pocket!

using smartphones.[3] However, another 2010 study found that 33 percent of teens would like to buy an iPhone.[4]

The draw of a smartphone is Internet access and the ability to do a variety of things with the phone. A smartphone can be your music player, calendar, to-do list, contacts list, gaming console, and e-book reader, and it can do most of the things that you do on a regular computer, including online shopping and checking e-mail. You can use it to chat, leaving texting behind. You can also call people!

Texting

Texting has become the primary use of the cell phone by teens: 72 percent of all teens send texts, according to a Pew Internet study.[5] The older you are, the more likely it is that you have a cell phone and therefore use it to text your friends

QR Codes

You see them everywhere these days: black and white boxes of pixels. They're showing up on billboards and in magazines. What are they? Website links!

Companies can use these barcodes for a variety of purposes. Ones that you see highlighted in advertising offer you a direct link to their websites. Using your smartphone and a QR code—reading app, you can take a photo of the barcode, and it automatically loads the website.

and family. Adults are texting too, with more than 50 percent of mobile phone–owning adults texting an average of 10 messages per day. Teens use texting to chat with friends, ask quick questions, and coordinate when meeting in person.

In addition to maintaining relationships with friends, texting is useful in communicating with parents and other family members. Texting teens are more likely to be in touch with their parents throughout the day than were older generations, without the ability to text. It could be news about a test at school or a check-in about a change in plans. It's less embarrassing to get a text from mom than a phone call that interrupts your time with friends. Texting allows teens to

Statistics on Mobile Internet Use in 2011

- 200 million active users access Facebook through their mobile device, according to Facebook.
- 21 percent of teens get their Internet solely from their phone, according to Pew Internet.
- 45 percent of smartphone owners end their day checking the mobile Internet, according to mobileYouth.com.

> ## Statistics on Texting
>
> - 80 percent of teenage cell phone owners sent texts regularly in 2011, according to Pew Internet.
> - 50 percent of teens sent at least 50 text messages a day in 2010, according to Pew Internet.
> - 1.5 hours of texting per day was spent by teens in 2010, according to a Kaiser Family Foundation study.

get some distance from their parents while still being in touch and having parents only a quick call away if they're needed.

Texting can give an alternative to face-to-face talks, and it can often be easier to bring up a tough subject or express feelings that are hard to say out loud. Talk to your parents (or, hey, send them a text) to make sure they understand your intention when having heavier conversations via text, and pay attention to the times when a face-to-face conversation is the better course. And be sure to thank your parents for learning and using your preferred method of communication.

Sexting

"You can't stop people if they're set out to [sext], but be aware of the consequences. Teenagers will rarely stay with their 16-year-old boyfriend/girlfriend for the rest of their lives, and should a nasty break up occur and any 'private' images be sent out in spite, it would be pretty embarrassing. This happened to a girl in my year who . . . sent some photos to her boyfriend of the time, who then last year showed them around to people in my year. It wasn't particularly pleasant for her." —Grace, age 16

Sexting is the act of sending sexually explicit messages or photographs via text messaging, either through your phone or online. The concerns for this behavior among teens are many: adults fear teenage sexuality; teens may be pressured into

What Teens Are Saying

"I text my friends and my mom often and it's a good way for me to contact people. I typically send around 300 hundred texts a day. I don't text in class very often, but I do when it is necessary." —Annie, age 16

"It's a good thing, I think, for teens to text. I have a friend who lives in New Jersey that I would never talk to if not for texting." —Ava, age 16

"I understand why people think that teenagers use [texting] too often. Cell phones aren't allowed to be on during school hours at my school, but I've visited a school where kids just had them out texting in class, and that was a little much in my opinion." —Averill, age 18

"I have a cell phone, I send maybe around 100 texts a day, I don't text often, only to talk to my loved ones that live far away." —Bow, age 20

"I think teens using phones the way we do is very good and bad. I love being able to talk to my girlfriend all day but often if we were just to talk on the phone at night it would help advance the trust in the relationship and help us be good friends as well as just 'lovey-dovey' to each other." —Jack S., age 17

"I'm not too dependent on my phone. I have a flip-phone, not one of those fancy-shmancy iPhones or Droids, haha." —Niki, age 15

"If it's important, they'll call me." —Jack C., age 14

taking photos they're not comfortable with; the photos may be forwarded to more than the intended recipient; and there may even be legal ramifications related to child pornography. Interestingly, adults are more likely to sext than teens—a 2010 Pew Internet study found that only 4 percent of teens sent sexts while 6 percent

What Adults Are Saying

"My 17-year-old daughter, Addie, and I text several times a day, on topics ranging from the logistical (Me: 'Did you remember to pack your tennis racket?' Addie: 'Yes, and can we pleeeeaaasssee go to cvs after school? I need makeup!') to the profound (Me: 'I'm sorry I yelled at you.' Addie: 'Me too')."
—Kate Tuttle on Boston.com[6]

of adults have done so, although other studies have found teen use may be as high as 20 percent.[7]

Why do it? Sex is high in the minds of teens as they grow up, whether they're ready for it or not. There are many stories of couples where one is pushing the other to go further than he or she is comfortable with, and sexting can be part of that. For some, it can be a status symbol. Having a naked picture of your boyfriend or girlfriend in your phone can make it seem that you're more sexually active than you really are, giving you status among your peers. If you are in a relationship where sexting is a possibility, have a frank conversation with your partner about your feelings. If he or she isn't willing to listen to and respect your beliefs, do you want to be in that relationship anyway?

The bottom line is that you can control how photos of yourself are treated only while they remain in your possession, so never send them away (or take them!) in the first place. Also, never forward an uncomfortable text message, and let your friends know you won't participate in such activities. The best thing to do with a sext is hit *Delete*.

Texting While Driving

One of the biggest dangers of texting is being distracted while you're doing it. This is especially dangerous if you're driving at the time! The National Highway

Traffic Safety Administration says that 16 percent of fatal accidents involved distracted driving, killing nearly 5,500 Americans in 2009. Texting while driving increases your risk of getting in an accident by 23 times! Add that teens are 3 times more likely to die in a car crash than adult drivers, and the odds are stacked against you.

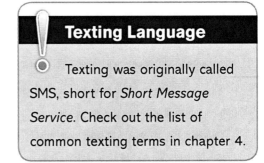

Texting Language

Texting was originally called SMS, short for *Short Message Service*. Check out the list of common texting terms in chapter 4.

One study found that texting while driving was significantly more dangerous than driving drunk. *Car and Driver* magazine conducted an experiment in 2009 to test how long it took a driver to hit the brakes when a red light came on. Don't worry—they did this on a closed race track with nothing dangerous to hit. At 70 miles per hour, when the driver was sober and paying attention, he braked in 0.54 seconds, and the study measured where he stopped. When he was drunk, he stopped 4 feet farther down the track. Reading an e-mail added 36 feet, and sending a text added 70 feet!

The danger of this practice has become prominent in the media, and there are plenty of campaigns to convince people to stop texting on the road. One study found that 89 percent of Americans think texting while driving should be illegal,

Suggestions for Cell Phones in the Car

1. Turn it off! If you can't keep your hands off it, turn it off for the drive.
2. Tell your friends. If you don't feel safe while they're driving, talk to them about it.
3. Pull over. If you must take that call, do it from the side of the road.
4. Your passenger may be happy to answer that text for you.

What Teens Are Saying

"I also do not text and drive. I think that it is a bad choice and very dangerous."
—Annie, age 16

"Teenagers aren't always the best drivers in the first place, and it's not a good thing to add in another distraction, but I'm definitely not advocating starting another fear-mongering campaign designed to scare teens into not texting. That doesn't work." —Averill, age 18

"In my opinion it shouldn't be just teens that are singled out for texting and driving, it should be everyone." —Bow, age 20

"Not only teens—but anyone should be careful with their phone and driving. I know my Dad texts and talks on the phone while driving all the time. He's stopped for the most part now, but it is a very dangerous thing—and after seeing some of the injuries people have obtained from car accidents when my school went to a RTA Road Safety excursion . . . I was absolutely horrified."
—Grace, age 16

"The idea of texting and driving is just dumb. Maybe it's because I was taught to drive without any distractions but obviously using your head and hand to type out a message on a tiny keyboard, or even worse no keyboard, is flat out stupid." —Jack S., age 17

"The dad of one of my friends texts while he drives, and I've refused rides from him once I found that out. Texting is a distraction, and if I'm putting my life in someone else's hands, I'd like for them to be 100 percent focused!"
—Niki, age 15

"Texting and driving is bad for sure. I think you should just follow the rules. When you know the consequences then why do it?" —Priyanka, age 15

"Don't text and drive. That's just stupid." —Ava, age 16

"When it comes to texting and driving, I think that is only a danger if you don't know what you are doing. I think the issue comes when people are not careful with how they do it. If you text while sitting at a stop light you are not putting anyone at danger. I feel that by banning it has actually made the roads more unsafe. The people who were unsafe doing it in the first place will still do it, except they now have to hide it in their laps. This creates more driving time with your eyes not on the road." —Adam, age 17

"I think it's good for teens to have the ability to call someone in an emergency, but they should never call or text anyone when they should be paying attention." —Jack C., age 14

but 66 percent of those people admitted to doing it themselves, showing how difficult it is to stop. Many states are writing laws about texting while driving, and some are addressing talking on the phone while driving as well.

Mobile Apps

Smartphones allow you to download applications, or *apps*, to use on your phone. Since mobile is the future of computing, gaming, and communication, the app

Statistics on Mobile Apps in 2010

10: The average number of apps used by youth on their phones, according to mobileYouth.com

7 hours, 13 minutes: Time spent watching video on a mobile phone by teens (that's twice as much as adults!), according to Nielsen

What Teens Are Saying

"I don't like how addicting the apps are, because they are pointless and waste my time."

—Annie, age 16

business is booming. The most popular apps are programs that allow your phone to have other functions, such as watching TV shows or reading books. Playing games is by far the biggest use.

Your smartphone has an app that allows you to browse what is available, including a way to search for free apps. To find out which ones you absolutely must have, ask your friends what they can't live without. You can also search online for *best apps*. It may help to add the name of your platform to the search to get specialized results: *best apps android*.

E-readers

The ability to read a book on your phone, computer, or e-reader (think Nook or Kindle) is another thing of the future just now getting popular. While many people bemoan the loss of the physical book—there is something about the physical act of reading that an e-reader cannot duplicate—there are many benefits. Many college students are choosing an e-reader and digital books over heavy textbooks. Students of all ages comment that their backpacks are so much lighter when the textbooks are in an e-reader. The text is keyword searchable, and often you can highlight sections or add notes as you read. It's also useful when going on a long trip where having multiple books to read for pleasure would be a hardship in your luggage. Having your textbook available on the Internet means that you don't have to haul it home to do your math homework every night.

Libraries offer free digital books as well. Check out your school and public library websites to find out what they have to offer. You don't have to have an e-reader, because many e-book companies offer an app or program to download that allows you to use the book on your device or computer, regardless of what you own.

> ### ! Bubble Ball
>
> Bubble Ball is a physics-based puzzle game app that was created by 14-year-old Robert Nay, who wrote over 4,000 lines of code because his friends suggested he could make a better app. Nay told *The Guardian*, "There were some times when I felt like, 'Can people seriously do this?' It seemed impossible. But then there were times when things just worked and I would be like: 'Maybe I can actually do this.'"[8] Bubble Ball was downloaded over 300,000 times in its first week and was declared the top app in the United States just 1 week later! Nay has plans to release more games and is considering charging for the next one.

Not all books are available in digital format, but more and more are added every day. Publishers are beginning to automatically release a digital format of books at the same time that they print them. The cost of the book is decreased, due to a lack of paper and glue, but e-books still cost money because you are also paying for the work that went into writing them.

Free Ringtones

"I usually take music from my computer and turn it into ringtones." —Jack C., age 14

You know that movie scene where a group of people are standing around and a cell phone rings and all of them reach for their phone? Customizing your ringtones is necessary when you're surrounded by friends who have cell phones too. But where do you get the interesting unique ringtones? You see the ads for free ringtones everywhere, on practically every website, but those advertisements are often much more trouble than what you wanted for one simple ringtone. The better way to get ringtones is to use free ringtone websites, such as PhoneZoo.com and Myxer.com. Search for *free ringtones* and ask your friends which they use.

Amanda Hocking, e-Book Author

Twenty-six-year-old Amanda Hocking has sold over a million copies of her 17 novels without the help of a publisher or even a literary agent. Before April 2010, she had never managed to sell a single copy despite having them for sale in multiple places. Then she decided to give Kindle, Amazon's e-book reader, a try. She said, "Worst case scenario, nobody would read them, and that's what was happening anyway."[9] Within a few weeks, she was selling a minimum of 1,000 books a month! A year later, she is a millionaire and has been picked up by a major (print) publisher.

Hocking is modest in her success. She said, "When I stopped judging myself, that was actually a huge turning point in my whole personality. I realized that it's OK to like things like 'The Breakfast Club' even though it's not critically acclaimed. It's OK to like the Muppets. I'd always been a closet lame person. I think I became cooler when I stopped trying to be cool."[10]

These sites allow users to create and share ringtones and wallpapers. Be aware that each ringtone or picture you receive counts as a multimedia text and normal charges will apply. You can also buy ringtones from your phone company and sites such as iTunes. The charge typically shows up on your next phone bill, so be sure to have your parents' permission before making the purchase.

Free ringtone sites are often set up as social networks, allowing you to friend other users and tag your favorite items. Regular rules of online friendship can get lost because it is acceptable to friend a user who has uploaded a lot of quality ringtones that match your preferences. Since these users are strangers, be cautious about what information you put on your profile and give in messages.

Once you've created a registration and set up your phone to receive texts from the website, you can search for songs and sounds, preview them, and send them to your phone. Searching these sites can be difficult because it involves searching the tags added to the ringtones by the creator. When searching for a specific ringtone,

---

! Ringtones Adults Can't Hear

Search the free ringtone websites for "high pitch" to find tones that are so highly pitched that many adults can't even hear them. Because you are younger and have better hearing, you can hear them. Experiment with these tones if you have issues with hearing your phone but your parents request that you keep the ringer off. Be careful though—some adults can hear them!

---

it is best to try different keywords and not combine too many words in one search. For more general searches, consider using a broad term, such as *funny* or *music*, to browse a variety of results. These websites will also have ranked lists of the top ringtones or photos for you to browse, letting you see what other users have downloaded the most.

Many free ringtone websites allow you to record your voice or upload an MP3 file and make a ringtone out of it. The best sites, such as PhoneZoo, will allow you to choose a portion of the file to be in the ringtone and how long the segment will be. This allows you to grab that one good verse or sound and create a new ringtone of it. It's best to use your highest-quality files when making ringtones, since any background noise can drown out the desired sound. Also, making a ringtone from a copyrighted file, such as a song you bought online, is legal only if you don't share it with anyone. These sites will allow you to keep such files private—don't share them with your friends either.

Should Mobile Phones Be Allowed at School?

"I use this site called 'epic fail,' when I have wifi, I download a few pics to my ipod so that I can show my friends. One time, I was using this site in class, and when the teacher saw it, instead of confiscating [my phone], saw the funny pic and told me to put it away." —Jack C., age 14

What Adults Are Saying

"Handheld devices like cell phones, iPhones, BlackBerrys and iTouch are beginning to offer applications that enhance classroom learning by engaging kids to use tools they are constantly using anyway." —Daniel A. Domenech, executive director of the American Association of School Administrators[11]

"Teens view mobile as a right; if they are not in the classroom, they expect to be able to use their phones otherwise on campus. They view mobile phone policies as a barometer of how their schools respect them and view their maturity." —Ms. Twixt on YPulse.com[12]

Many people worry that cell phones in class cause a distraction and encourage cheating. In one study, 35 percent of teens admitted to using their cell phone to cheat in school, and 65 percent said others in their school cheated with them. Cell phones can also be used in bullying and making plans for mischief. Therefore, 69 percent of schools ban cell phones during the school day (but 63 percent of teens use them anyway).

The news isn't all bad though. Principal Michael Bregy of Harry D. Jacobs High School in Algonquin, Illinois, gave his personal cell phone number out to his entire student body at the start of the fall semester in 2009. He received 100 texts in the first week and had to upgrade his phone plan to keep up. That Thanksgiving, many of his students said, "Thanks for caring."[13]

Schools are realizing that the bans aren't working, and instead, teachers are finding more ways to incorporate mobile uses into their lesson plans, in addition to the other technology already in the classroom. Cell phones can be an excellent way of getting students interested and engaged while teaching skills they will need after graduation.

Notes

1. Natasha Lomas, "Q&A: Kurzweil on Tech as a Double-Edged Sword," November 19, 2008, http://news.cnet.com/8301-11386_3-10102273-76.html.
2. PCMag.com, "Definition of: Smartphone," 2011, www.pcmag.com/encyclopedia_term/0,2542,t=Smartphone&i=51537,00.asp.
3. Marketing Charts, "US Youth Have Higher Smartphone Penetration Than Adults," January 12, 2011, www.marketingcharts.com/uncategorized/us-youth-have-higher-smartphone-penetration-than-adults-15665/.
4. Taly Weiss, "Mobile Web Will Be Catching Up with Text Messaging with More Teens Owning Smartphones," November 17, 2010, www.trendsspotting.com/blog/?p=2014.
5. Amanda Lenhart et al., "Teens and Mobile Phones," April 20, 2010, http://pewInternet.org/Reports/2010/Teens-and-Mobile-Phones/Chapter-2/Part-1.aspx?r=1.
6. Kate Tuttle, "I Love You, Now Do Your Homework," *Boston Globe*, September 11, 2010, www.boston.com/community/moms/articles/2010/09/11/texting_can_distance_teens_from_parents_but_it_can_also_lead_to_better_communication/.
7. Amanda Lenhart, "Teens, Adults and Sexting: Data on Sending/Receiving Sexually Suggestive Nude or Nearly Nude Photos by Americans," October 23, 2010, www.pewInternet.org/Presentations/2010/Oct/Teens-Adults-and-Sexting.aspx.
8. Sam Jones, "Angry Birds Knocked Off Perch by Bubble Ball," *The Guardian*, January 18, 2011, www.guardian.co.uk/technology/2011/jan/18/angry-bird-bubble-ball-itunes.
9. Tonya Plank, "Meet Mega Bestselling Indie Heroine Amanda Hocking," January 5, 2011, www.huffingtonpost.com/tonya-plank/meet-mega-bestselling-ind_b_804685.html.
10. Strawberry Saroyan, "Storyseller," *New York Times*, June 17, 2011, www.nytimes.com/2011/06/19/magazine/amanda-hocking-storyseller.html.
11. Daniel A. Domenech, "Harnessing Kids' Tech Fascination," *School Administrator* 9, no. 66 (2009), www.aasa.org/SchoolAdministratorArticle.aspx?id=6884.
12. Ms. Twixt, "Guest Post: Mobile Safety, Digital Literacy and Media Myths," December 15, 2010, www.ypulse.com/guest-post-mobile-safety-literacy-myths-%E2%80%94-insights-from-fccs-generation-mobile-forum.
13. Alex Johnson, "Some Schools Rethink Ban on Cell Phones," February 3, 2010, www.msnbc.msn.com/id/35063840/.

HOW TO SAVE THE WORLD

"The biggest contribution that you have is your voice. Your ability to speak up and speak out about things, but in order to do that you have to know about them. Social media is an incredible way to get it out there fast. That's really what I use it for."
—*Monique Coleman, actress from High School Musical*[1]
"Volunteering is a two-way street, no matter how much I give, I get something in return."
—*Sally O'Brien, age 18, on DoSomething.org*[2]

In 1960, four black college students made a stand by sitting at the "whites only" lunch counter at Woolworths. Within days, tens of thousands of their peers—primarily college students—were standing up for their rights all across the southern United States. Word of mouth moved across the country, town by town. They did this without the convenience and speed of social media. Fast forward to the revolt in Iran in 2009, where people used Twitter to get the word out and drum up support. There was also a dramatic increase in the number of text messages sent to Iranian cell phones during the revolt, nearly doubling over the normal use.[3] The majority of that support came from the Western world, but the effort worked—84 percent of Iranians voted in the resulting election.

So what does that mean for you? Studies show that youth who participate in online communities are more likely to be interested in civic or political topics and are more likely to hear about different political views, therefore giving them the chance to make educated decisions when forming their own opinions. They

Find your volunteer opportunities online to make real-life friends.

are also more likely to participate in volunteer opportunities for charities and politicians in real life.

People join a fight they care about. Most people find a fight to care about via word of mouth, from friends and acquaintances. Social media sites such as Facebook and Twitter allow you to keep in contact with those acquaintances and to share what you feel strongly about. Providing knowledge can give them something to fight for, which they in turn spread to their friends and acquaintances. Facilitation of groups of people over social media allows even smaller movements to find support.

The biggest issue with coordinated effort for a cause is having a leader. A large network of people will not be able to make decisions in a responsible and timely manner. Someone, often a corporation, needs to step forward and tell the network how to accomplish its goal. Organizations seeking to help others are often looking for that leader within their volunteers. Participating in these organizations can give you tools to improve yourself as well as helping others.

Some Statistics about Volunteerism in 2011[4]

- 72 percent of high school and college students have a specific cause they invest in
- 79 percent volunteer regularly
- 50 percent regularly donate money to their cause, at an average of $80 per year

Finding an organization that you care about can be difficult. Most likely it's something you'll stumble across unexpectedly. If you are searching, start with your friends and their friends. Ask people you respect what they think matters most, and consider how their answers fit in with your own opinions and desires.

If you are interested in helping out locally (or don't have available transportation), try the website for your town or neighborhood associations.

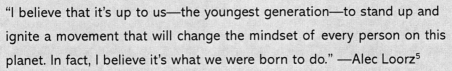

Alec Loorz, Climate Change Activist

"I believe that it's up to us—the youngest generation—to stand up and ignite a movement that will change the mindset of every person on this planet. In fact, I believe it's what we were born to do." —Alec Loorz[5]

Four years ago, Alec Loorz found his passion: global warning. At age 16, he proclaims, "I've spent my entire teenaged life traveling around giving speeches and presentations about climate change because I believe my generation was born to solve this crisis."[6] In 2011, Alec led a group of youth and lawyers in a suit against the United States for failing to protect the earth's atmosphere. He also led youth to march in cities across the world to spread global climate change awareness in the iMatter March.

> **! Mimi Ausland, Kibble Provider**
>
> Mimi Ausland volunteered at an animal shelter and saw a need for good, quality food for the animals. She launched a website, www.freekibble.com, where trivia questions answered (correctly or incorrectly) each day provide a donation of 10 pieces of kibble. In 3 years, she has donated 554 million pieces of kibble— over 740,000 pounds of pet food.

Search for the word *volunteer* to see if any opportunities are listed. Look around at your school to see what projects are happening. Also, visit your public library and ask the librarians for help finding volunteer opportunities. They may maintain a list or have information on local agencies which use volunteers.

There are websites that can help you find a cause of your own. DoSomething .org "helps young people rock causes they care about"[7] because it believes that "using the power of the web and pop culture [can] help young people change the world."[8] The website lists causes and explains how to help, including guides to get started.

YouthNoise.com is another site for teens to find worthy causes. Sparked.com provides volunteer opportunities that you can do from your computer, usually in just a few minutes.

The social network Jumo.com wants to connect you to the organizations that are working to change the world. Once you create your profile, you can follow organizations that interest you, connect with friends who have similar interests, and share your own projects.

MTV's Act (http://act.mtv.com/) is a blog about people making a difference— and not all of them are famous. This is a great website to use when you're looking for your personal cause.

When you are considering giving time, money, or even just interest to a certain charity, it's best to know something about that company. Try Charity Navigator

Chad Bullock, Antitobacco Activist

After losing a family member to lung cancer, 18-year-old Chad Bullock decided to create a community that would reject big tobacco companies. He started a movement on DoSomething.org and won $100,000 in 2008. He used the money to start a website, http://hellochange.org, which shares information about all facets of antitobacco activism.

(www.charitynavigator.org) to get that information. It evaluates and rates major charities, with 4 stars meaning *exceptional* and no stars meaning *exceptionally poor*. These ratings are based on how the charity does compared to charities in the same service field. The site also provides information regarding where the donated money goes and what level of accountability the organization has, as well as news articles and reviews from people who have donated to the charity. You can browse Charity Navigator to find new charities or causes as well.

YouTube Projects That Are Saving the World

"The power of YouTube lies in its capacity to create connections," explains Shawn Ahmed, the activist behind the Uncultured Project. It forms "connections between people and connections between communities [that are stronger] than

Some Statistics about Teen Volunteers in 2010

- 79 percent of American girls have given food or clothing to charity, according to the United Nations Foundation
- 56 percent of teens volunteer for charitable causes (compared to 46 percent of adults), according to DoSomething.org

---

What Teens Are Saying

"I think having [charity] organizations online is a good idea. It allows people to take part in small things that they can make a difference in from their very own computers. It raises an awareness of certain issues, and as the Internet is such a widely accessible database of information—finding out about the issues which the charities are trying to spread a message about is only too easy. I fully support it." —Grace, age 16

"I don't trust them." —Daniel, age 17

---

pen pals, and [stronger] than just exchanging e-mails or Facebook pokes. It's a way of kind of seeing and connecting visually, auditorily, everything."[9] Here are some ways that people are using YouTube to make the world a better place.

Nerdfighters are self-proclaimed nerds declaring war on "world suck," led by brothers John and Hank Green. Once a year, Nerdfighters band together for the Project for Awesome (www.projectforawesome.com/), creating videos promoting their favorite charities and making a concerted effort to get the videos to the top of YouTube's lists of popular videos. The 2010 Project for Awesome campaign raised over $100,000 for charity.

Gay rights activist Dan Savage launched the It Gets Better Project (www.youtube .com/itgetsbetterproject) in response to gay students committing suicide because of bullying. He started by posting a video of himself and his partner talking about how life gets better. People from around the world, gay and straight, famous and unknown, have recorded videos of their own to add to the message.

The Uncultured Project (http://uncultured.com) aims to raise awareness about Global Poverty by posting videos that share stories about people in third world countries. Leader Shawn Ahmed was surprised when people wanted to donate money to his cause. He explains, "It's my unplanned, unexpected, and 'uncultured' journey to make the world a better place—one meaningful difference at a time."[10]

Streetside Stories brings literacy and art to schools in San Francisco, giving students the ability to tell their own stories as well as learning useful skills. The stories are amazing: www.youtube.com/user/streetsidestoriessf.

Political Activism

Politicians are finding ways to use social media to get the word out about their campaigns as well as find volunteers to assist in their election. Barack Obama used social media to win the 2008 presidential election, using a variety of tools to spread his promises, fight negative comments from his opponent, and organize his followers at a local level. He also raised $6.5 million online, from 3 million donors, and at an average of only $80 a time. Obama's online team sent more than 1 billion e-mails and had 1 million people signed up via text. More than 2 million profiles were created on Obama's personal social network, plus another 3 million supporters on a variety of other networks. He and his team managed this feat by posting advertising every where they could find, analyzed the results, and spread the ads again. Chris Hughes, a member of Obama social media team, told the *Washington Post*, "What we've learned from this campaign is that there's huge

> **!** **Shauna Lynn Fleming, Soldier Letter Campaign Writer**
>
> ◉ Starting in her own school when she was a freshman, Shauna Lynn Fleming launched a letter-writing campaign for soldiers that grew into a government collaboration to send millions of letters to military personnel. A Million Thanks (http://amillionthanks.org/) has delivered over 5 million letters since 2009.

potential for people that haven't been involved in politics to discover that, yes, this is something that impacts me. Even before I joined the campaign, the fundamental premise was to help put the political process into people's own hands. That was the value from the start of the campaign, that was the value at the end of the campaign, and it's not going away."[11]

You can also use social media to educate yourself about political concerns. RockTheVote.org and Project Vote Smart (www.votesmart.org/) are websites dedicated to educating young voters. They provide a place to learn about and discuss candidates and issues.

Consumerism

Making wise choices about where you spend your money is one very powerful way that you and your friends can affect world change. Advertisements surround you in the online world, from ads in your favorite games to carefully placed logos and products in movies. Since you have learned to not even see those advertisements, the companies are getting more creative in how they make their product interesting to you. One way is to be involved in social media just as you are. They are walking a fine line—they have to inform you and create interest in their product or service without annoying you such that you block them.

Be wary of what companies you allow access to your personal information on your social media sites. Some of their ideas about how to keep your attention can

What Teens Are Saying

"I have friended a few companies, which will get me nice deals, and I like that. However, for the most part, I ignore ads. It would creep me out if a company responded to a post [I wrote] because that seems like they would be going too far into my personal life." —Annie, age 16

"If [companies] post something on my wall, I normally get rid of the permissions I gave them because it seems like I am just giving my social life away to scams." —Daniel, age 17

"I think that the advertisements are a waste of time. No one that I know does them, it's a waste of money." —Jake, age 13

be downright creepy. One airline checked the Facebook pages of their passengers who checked in at the airport via Foursquare and provided personalized gifts when they arrived on the plane. For instance, a passenger who was going to miss an important soccer match while he was traveling was gifted with a travel guide of his destination city with places he could watch the match highlighted. Is that good service or going too far?

One way that companies attempt to get your attention is by creating social media campaigns that are so awesome, they go viral. A video goes viral when people are sharing it widely, making it possible for millions of people to see it. The more the video is discussed on various social media platforms, the bigger the audience. There is no way of knowing what will and will not go viral, so companies are making their best guesses. One example of a viral advertising campaign was the Old Spice guy introduced during the Super Bowl in 2010. The commercial was entertaining and amusing, but it was the company's follow-up that really caught the world's attention. It had its spokesman, Isaiah Mustafa, make more

---

⚠ Teens Building Better Online Stores

When the creators of a new shopping site called PlumWillow were designing it, they turned to their audience for help. Over the course of a year, more than 20 high school girls worked with the company (for school credit) on how to make the website appealing and useful for their peers. Charlie Federman, the chairman of the company, told the *New York Times*, "Adults trying to recreate that are just asking for trouble because these kids are smart and sophisticated and know when something is phony."[12]

---

than 180 videos in response to questions people asked him online. In one video, he proposed marriage to one fan's girlfriend; she accepted. The advertising campaign was a success because it reached such a huge audience, and people remembered both the videos and the product.

Notes

1. DoSomethingU, "How to Use Social Media for Good," November 23, 2010, www.dosome thing.org/u/video/video-how-to-use-social-media-good.
2. Marguerite Marsh, "Teens Making a Difference," January 31, 2010, www.columbusparent .com/live/content/issue/stories/2010/02/01/teens-making-a-difference.html.
3. Doron Peskin, "Iranian Election Campaign Costs Millions," June 13, 2009, www.ynetnews .com/articles/0,7340,L-3730357,00.html.
4. Gwendolyn Radsch, "Green That Counts," May 13, 2011, www.mediapost.com/ publications/?fa=Articles.showArticle&art_aid=150335.
5. iMatter March, "iMatter March Intro," 2011, http://vimeo.com/20612203.
6. Alec Loorz, "Letter from Alec Loorz—Youth Leader," March 2011, http://imattermarch. org/.
7. DoSomething.org, "About Us," n.d., www.dosomething.org/about.
8. DoSomething.org, "Facts and Fun Stats about Do Something," n.d., www.dosomething.org/ about/stats-info.
9. Sarah Kessler, "5 YouTube Projects That Are Making a Difference," October 5, 2010, http:// mashable.com/2010/10/05/youtube-projects-social-good/.
10. Shawn Ahmed, "About Me," n.d., http://uncultured.com/about/.

11. Jose Antonio Vargas, "Obama Raised Half a Billion Online," *Washington Post*, November 20, 2008, http://voices.washingtonpost.com/44/2008/11/20/obama_raised_half_a_billion_on.html.

12. Jenna Wortham, "Turning Customers into Creators," *New York Times*, October 23, 2010, www.nytimes.com/2010/10/24/business/24ping.html.

HOMEMADE MOVIES: MANAGE YOUR VIDEOS

··

"I think online videos are awesome because they are free (mostly) and easy to get to."
—Jack C., age 14

One thing is clear to the Internet world: teens love videos! With the ability to make a video in every cell phone, personal videos are becoming more popular every day. Eighty-four percent of online Americans viewed at least one video online in October 2010, for a total of over 5.4 billion videos viewed. Companies are getting involved, making more than commercials for the teen audience.

The biggest player in this video world is YouTube.com, and its competition is tiny in comparison. YouTube is visited by around 18 million Americans per day, accounting for only 22 percent of its total visitors. Music videos are a major part of YouTube because it has a deal with 3 of the 4 major American music producers concerning where they will publish their music videos. The other major component of YouTube is amateur videos—anyone can create a video and post it for others to view. And you never know what will catch on and make it big.

There are other places to view videos. Social networking sites such as Facebook allow you to upload videos to share with your friends, which is much more private and controlled. Hulu.com is a television- and movie-sharing site created by 3 major television networks. Vimeo.com is intended for user-created content only and has different rules about what can be uploaded. Since Google owns both Vimeo and YouTube, much of Vimeo's content is available on YouTube too.

What Teens Are Saying

"I enjoy watching random stuff on YouTube." —Annie, age 16

"Good videos are great! Bad videos are very unhealthy for you. I got in trouble for watching some bad videos." —Jake, age 13

"I watch YouTube a lot, from daily news to music videos to just funny randomness." —Niki, age 15

"Many new artists have been discovered by record companies [through video sharing on YouTube]. Sometimes you can also just get a good laugh out of a video." —Adam, age 17

You can even watch television shows and movies online. Averill explains, "I also watch a lot of online television and movies, mostly through Hulu and Netflix. We got rid of our TV a few years ago, but with these kinds of sites it doesn't even matter. As a matter of fact most of my friends with televisions watch most of their TV online anyway, just because you can decide when to watch it." According to a Kaiser Family Foundation study published in 2009, teens spend 41 percent of their television viewing time online rather than in front of a television.

Videos on Social Networks

You can upload videos to your favorite social networking site. Look for a *video* tag on your main page or your profile. When you upload the video, it will ask you to give it a title, description, and privacy setting, and you can tag any friends who are in it. Videos work much the same way as photos—you can tag friends, and comment, share, and like them.

Some Stats about YouTube Videos in 2011, according to YouTube.com

- 2,000,000,000 videos watched on YouTube every day in 2011.
- 24 hours of YouTube video uploaded every minute, which is equal to 18,500 full-length Hollywood movie releases a day!

Videos on Video-Sharing Sites

Since YouTube is used more than any other video site, this chapter focuses on how to use it. YouTube is a social network with friends, links to channels, and ways to share and comment on the videos.

Start by creating an account with YouTube or logging in using your Google account. The *Sign in* or *Create account* buttons are on YouTube's main page toward the top. You have a profile page, which lists any updates to channels you've subscribed to, as well as channels that YouTube thinks you would like. It also lists featured videos (meaning that someone paid to have it come up, such as an advertisement) and videos that are currently becoming popular, or "trending."

Watching a video is as easy as pressing *Play*. YouTube also allows you to change the volume, the resolution, and the size of the viewing screen for each video. If the video is inappropriate, there is a button to have the staff review it. Never use that button in jest because it could get the channel owner banned!

There may be text content below the video that was added by the channel owner, which can provide an explanation for the video, plus tags and categories to make it easier to find when searching. You can also see the number of times that the video has been watched and, by clicking on the button next to the number, see statistics about how the video was watched and referred. It even gives information such as the age and gender of the watchers and what countries watch it the most.

The First Video on YouTube

The first video on YouTube was uploaded by founder Jawed Karim at 8:27 PM on Saturday, April 23, 2005. It is called "Me at the Zoo" and is 19 seconds of Karim talking about elephants at the San Diego Zoo. You can find it by searching YouTube for *me at the zoo*.

You can also comment on videos, read comments left by other viewers, and reply to or like/dislike the comments. The highest-rated comments are displayed just below the video. Some channel owners disable comments or have filters to stop spam and other annoying comments.

YouTube has a reputation for being one of the worst places when it comes to comments. Ariel says, "I dislike how some people use the comment area just to bash the things they don't like. Be respectful people! I'm not asking you to like it, just to realize that it has worth to someone and that the things you say can be hurtful."

YouTube comments are often rude, badly typed, and offensive, with 68 percent of comments including profanity. A common type of negative feedback insults the poster's sexuality, and as much as 23 percent of comments reference violence

What Teens Are Saying

"The only time I really use videos online is through YouTube. Just for music videos, finding out about something, watching my friends' guitar covers and sometimes makeup tutorials." —Grace, age 16

"I mainly watch videos on YouTube. I like the variety and the ability to see videos on there that you would never get to see anywhere else." —Ariel, age 18

What Teens Are Saying

"I think that YouTube is the worst social network site. You do a simple search for a music video, and you get something totally wrong and perverted. It is nasty!!" —Jake, age 13

"Other times I just go to YouTube and click on the browse and then just look at the music that was popular that day and listen to some of that music."
—Daniel, age 17

---

or sex. Because comments can be made anonymously, users feel they can get away with being just plain mean, and it has become part of the culture of YouTube.

In 2009, Google said that it is working on a way for users to control how they view comments, including the ability to filter. Until that is in place, however, it is up to users to restrict their own comment viewing as they see fit. It is possible to watch videos without ever scrolling down to see the comments or to only look at the top-rated comments without scrolling further. If you are ever uncomfortable with what you're reading in the comment section or watching in a video, move to another page immediately.

When you watch a video, you are given a few options for using YouTube's social network. You can

- like or dislike the video, the total of which is published so that others know how people generally feel about that video;
- add it to a playlist so that you can watch it later or watch it as part of a selection of videos that run in a row;
- share the video on a variety of other social networks, including Facebook, blog sites, or e-mail;
- put the best videos of a band's songs in a playlist for easy, continuous viewing (other users can watch your playlist too);
- add it to your list of favorite videos so that you can find it again easily;

Stopping and Starting!

When you're playing a video and it plays for a few seconds and then pauses over and over, you can fix it by stopping the video to let it load. If you let it load for a few minutes, it will run better. If it doesn't, turn off the sound and let it run however long it takes (while you do something else) and then replay it when it's done. If you have a slow computer, it's a good idea to only have one video loading at a time. Two videos loading will fight for bandwidth.

- subscribe to the video owner's channel so that your main page alerts you to any new videos uploaded to that channel; and
- click on the channel owner's name to find out what else he or she has uploaded, as well as more information about the person or organization.

YouTube uses these functions to determine the popularity of a video so that anything you click will be noted and used in suggesting the video to other people.

There is more to ranking than how many views a video has received. A video that has 200,000 views but no comments isn't going to rank very high in the culture of YouTube, where a video that has only 10,000 views but 2,000 people favorited it—now that's a popular video! It will get noticed by the YouTube ranking system and probably be featured on many users' main pages and recommendations, which will quickly raise the ranking. So comment, subscribe, and like videos every chance you get, and ask your friends to do the same.

Finding Videos

Most searching of videos is done to find a specific thing—a certain song or a clip that your friend recommends—or just surfing to find good videos and new things. These are two very different search goals.

Finding the Best Videos First

Feel like you are missing something? Want to be the first person in your social group to find the new big thing? Search for *top viral videos* in your favorite search engine to find sites that keep track of what's most popular.

Searching on Your Favorite Social Network

Videos listed on social networking sites are usually only available to friends, so you can start by going to your friends' profile pages and clicking on their video tabs. There isn't a way to just surf for videos.

Searching on YouTube

If you're looking for a specific video, put some keywords in the search box at the top of any page. If your search doesn't quite get you what you want, try different keywords. YouTube is smart enough to recognize similar terms and adjust your search automatically. For instance, the search for *cute kittens* brings up the same results as *cute cats*. It will also give you a few related searches to try.

You can use the search options to limit your search for things such as length, upload date, ratings, and view counts. You can also search specifically for channels or playlists.

Popular YouTube Channels

Looking for new YouTube celebrities to subscribe to? Search for *popular YouTube channels* in your favorite search engine to find articles and websites listing recent popular channels. Also, on YouTube's main page, scroll down for its most popular videos list, categorized by topic.

> ## Top Video of All Time!
>
> As of July 26, 2011, the most-watched video of all time in all categories is Justin Bieber's "Baby," with over 592.6 million views. What is the most watched video on the date you read this?

YouTube provides tools for browsing for a good video as well. Start by checking your list of videos recommended for you on your profile.

Click on *Browse* at the top, by the search box. All YouTube videos are given categories by the owner that are used in a keyword search. They are also used in the browse search, so you can limit the sort of video you're looking for without using keywords. For instance, cute kitten videos fall under *Pets and Animals*, while music videos fall under *Music*. Then scroll down to find lists of videos most viewed today in each category and overall.

Scroll way down to find the *Trending Topics* box, which gives the most-searched keywords for that category. The bigger and bolder a word, the more it is searched. Click on the words to repeat that search.

You can also use YouTube Charts to find currently popular videos. As of 2011, YouTube doesn't provide a direct link, so go straight there at www.youtube.com/charts. You can customize the list for most viewed, most discussed, most favorited, and more. You can also limit to a certain category and tell it what period to use. YouTube also as a comment search at www.youtube.com/comment_search, which you can use to see what comments are highest rated.

On the Internet

Most search engines include a video search that you can use if YouTube isn't working for you. It works the same way—put keywords in the search and see what comes up. Search engines will find YouTube videos, but they will also find videos from the other video-sharing sites as well as videos loaded on web pages. If you prefer a certain video site be given priority in your search, add the name to the search terms. For instance, *cute kittens Vimeo.*

Your Own Videos

It is likely that you carry a video recorder inside your phone. Have you considered making a video of your own? At the very least, it can be a lasting impression of your life right now, which you may appreciate having in 30 years. At the very most, you could become famous!

Being Safe and Private in Your Videos

Creating videos can accidentally give a view into your personal life that is best left offline. Be very careful about what you post online, in videos as well as other media.

Think about what you will say in a video before filming, and don't hesitate to refilm a portion if you don't like what you said. The rules of not getting too personal online apply in videos too. For instance, watch your backgrounds. Are there identifying school posters, pieces of mail, or family photos behind you while you film your video? Plan a backdrop that is appropriate for the video and also neutral.

Before posting a video, watch it with the eye of a stranger to see what personal information you might be inadvertently giving away. Do this before you post— because everything on the Internet is permanent!

Making Your Video

The simplest homemade video happens when you catch something funny or cool while recording. Crop the video to just the funny bit and you're done. You can also

That's My Take

Pima County (Arizona) Public Library worked with teens to create films that promote books and reading. Groups work together to create book trailers, which are posted on the library's website: www.library.pima.gov/teens/trailers/. Craig McBrine was 15 when he led his group to create a video about Elie Wiesel's *Night*, a story about the author's journey through the Holocaust. Craig was kind enough to answer some questions about the project and his experience.

Q: How did you get involved in the That's My Take project?

A: I was on the library's website, and I noticed the trailers. I was instantly intrigued. I saw that they were taking submissions to become part of this program. I knew with the right ideas and the right people, we could make a trailer compelling enough to make teens want to read that certain book.

Q: Why did you choose *Night*?

A: I thought, what better book could I choose to get a message across to teens? Something that digs *that* deep into people's emotions would make a great trailer and would definitely make people want to read the book.

Q: How did the project work?

A: We met pretty much every week with the mentors and went over how we enjoyed the book and how we want to make it appealing for others to read.

create more complex videos, even taking it to the level of filmmaker. This requires planning, acting, and significantly more editing. Check to see if your school has a video club or class you could join for assistance.

Editing a video can be very easy if you have the right programs on your computer. Windows comes with a program called Microsoft Movie Maker, which has been reviewed as one of the best free editing software programs available. If you have a Mac, look for Apple iMovie, as it may have come with your operating

The whole thing was a brilliantly exciting and exhilarating process from beginning to end, even amidst any difficulties we encountered.

Q: What advice do you have for people working in groups on a project?

A: If you have a cooperative team in a creative project such as this, it shines through in your finished project. You *need* to be able to know how to work in a group and make the best of it. You *need* to be able to yield to someone else's idea, even if you are completely convinced your way is the best way. You also *need* to be able to be assertive enough not to get trampled on by everyone else and their ideas. Finding the careful, delicate balance between those things is the most important thing to know when working in a group. That is definitely something I learned.

Q: Has the project made a difference in anything you've done since?

A: I learned quite a bit about the filmmaking process and all the work that goes into it from the initial idea to the final product. I've also mentioned it in job applications how I have worked with groups before and know how to manage myself in a business environment such as that.

Q: What advice do you have for other teens?

A: If you are presented with an opportunity to express yourself in some creative outlet, go for it. It is a very rewarding experience, and the lessons and values you learn from it are worth everything in the world. One last piece of advice that many people gave me that has helped me get through quite a few things: "Suck it up."

system. YouTube has a list of apps that you can download for free to assist in your moviemaking at www.youtube.com/create. There are other programs available online for free, so ask your friends for suggestions or search online for *free video editing software.* All these programs should come with a help file and online support if you have trouble figuring something out.

Friends can help you film your videos.

What Teens Are Saying

"I make 'how to' videos. It feels good when I upload a new video that I am proud of." —Daniel, age 17

"I think videos online are a good thing, but you have to be careful with what you include in them if uploading personal videos. Or, just don't be filmed doing something that you don't want the world to be able to access." —Grace, age 16

Vlogging

Vlogging—short for *video blogging*—is a personal journal kept on video and posted on either a blog site or a video site. It is a very popular category on YouTube, and some vlogs are very entertaining and interesting. Creating a vlog is as simple as turning on the camera and telling about your day or something that interests you. Most vloggers shoot a lot of talking and then edit it into a short video (around 4 minutes). Just talking to an invisible viewer can be boring, so vloggers use interesting cuts, such as moving closer to the camera to give a side comment or shifting back and forth on the screen to create interest.

Going Viral

Greyson Chance was 13 years old in April 2010 when he posted a video of himself singing a cover of Lady Gaga's "Paparazzi" on YouTube. His older brother wrote a letter to Ellen DeGeneres suggesting that she watch it. She says it only had about 10,000 views at that point, despite being featured on two social news sites. DeGeneres liked Greyson's performance so much that she invited him to perform on her talk show, arranged for him to receive a phone call from Lady Gaga (his "number one inspiration"[1]), and then opened her own recording label so that she could produce an album with him.

Tips for Making a Good Film

- The first step is a have a story outline with a beginning, middle, and end. All good stories have these parts.
- Plan ahead—write a script, plan your locations, consider wardrobe and props.
- Use good equipment—the better the camera, the better the quality of the video. Also, use a tripod to get steady shots.
- Cast the film with friends, especially if they can act well. Give them a voice in making changes.
- Have the actors rehearse several times, including how they will move while they talk.
- Film the most difficult scenes first, to get them out of the way.
- Don't move your camera around or zoom a lot. Excessive movement takes away from the actors. Do use different angels on the same subject to give interesting changes.
- Be aware of background noise because it will get recorded too. Plan to shoot video in a place that has appropriate background noise for the scene.
- Once it's done, make copies of the DVD for all the participants.

Chance went from being a musically gifted but normal sixth grader to being a YouTube star with a record deal in just a few months. He is now releasing his own songs, is sharing managers with Madonna and Lady Gaga, and has left school to focus on his music. "This is my dream and I'm living it," Greyson says on his website, "I've never wanted to do anything else except write songs and perform them."[2]

While this kind of rocket to fame only happens to a handful of people, there are things you could do to help yourself—or your friends—along the way. Greyson Chance's brother wrote a letter to a famous person asking her to look into this video. That's a very simple thing you can do too!

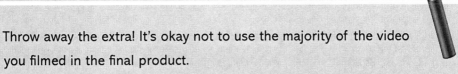

Tips for Editing Your Film

- Throw away the extra! It's okay not to use the majority of the video you filmed in the final product.
- Keep your scenes short, except when there is exciting action going on.
- Keep your overall film short. It is customary to keep videos to 2 to 4 minutes.
- Switch up the order of the scenes. Remember: you don't have to film in order, and you don't have to present the order in which you filmed.
- Be cautious of using effects during transitions between scenes. Most of the time, a simple change of scenery is good enough.
- Put some uncopyrighted music behind any scenes that have no relevant sound.
- Once you're done, go back and try to cut some more, especially in parts that seem long. Have someone with an unbiased eye view it and give you constructive feedback.

"The goal for marketing types in the Internet age is a 'viral' ad campaign. You pull off some publicity stunt, there's tons of coverage on the Internet, you wind up with millions of eyeballs for virtually no cost,"[3] explains Mark Hill, a writer for Cracked.com. One of the best viral campaigns was the advertising for the movie *The Blair Witch Project*. The reason that it succeeded was that people were never sure if it was real or not. The videos were said to be recovered video of teens falling victim to supernatural forces. It was scary and vague. Made with a budget of only a few thousand dollars, the movie is one of the most profitable movies of all time.

However, viral marketing campaigns don't always work out. For example, Tele2, a phone company in Latvia, published supposedly amateur video of a meteorite crashing in farmland one night, causing much excitement. In the light of

What about Copyright?

If you post copyrighted material online, you will be held accountable. In 2010, a federal court decided that YouTube was not liable for copyrighted videos on the site. The judge said that it is up to the owner of the copyright to inform YouTube of any illegal material, which YouTube must remove. YouTube told *Variety*, "This is an important victory not just for us, but also for the billions of people around the world who use the web to communicate and share experiences with each other."[4]

day, experts immediately saw that the crater was manmade. Tele2 later agreed to reimburse the country for the expense of sending military personnel and scientists to the site of the crater. Arguably, the hoax did have the desired effect of creating something new and interesting to talk about, mainly to distract attention from the country's economic crisis at the time, although how that relates to telephone service is unknown. The only real winner in this story is the landowner who charged all visitors $2 to see the crater.

YouTube videos have an average lifespan of just 6 days. That doesn't leave a very big window to make your video famous. The first thing is to have a good video, something well made that is interesting, funny, or exciting. It should be unique and not an obvious copy from some other popular video. It also needs to be of interest to a wide audience of people; cute kitten videos are infamous for being popular online because everyone loves a cute kitten! Make sure your thumbnail is the best possible image from the video; ideally, it is intriguing enough to make someone click on it. Make the video easy to find, with a catchy title, description, and appropriate tags.

Most important, make absolutely sure there is nothing copyrighted in the video—no logos on your clothes or in the background—and use only royalty-

Some Tips for Vlogging Content

- Be funny!
- Be current and cool.
- Have a script or key points planned—rambling with no point is bad.
- Do video responses to other videos, telling why you like them.
- Be relevant—tell about breaking news and what you think about it.
- Do something crazy and daring (but safe).
- Rant! Those who agree will love you; those who don't will watch to disagree.
- Make your message into a song, best if you wrote the music as well as the lyrics.

free music. YouTube has made it clear that it will not feature a video that could possibly get it in trouble. Copyright is an easy thing for YouTube to watch. Also, keep it clean. If YouTube puts an 18 rating on it—meaning, only those over 18 can watch—it's unlikely that it will feature the video.

Once you post your video, you need to advertise it like crazy. Get it on every blog, forum, e-mail list, and website you know. Have your friends share the video on Facebook and any other social networking site they use. Once it's posted on all those places, comment on every posting, but do it honestly so that people realize you're the creator. Encourage people to like, comment, and subscribe, as those are key factors in determining rank on video sites.

Even with all this hard work, it's unlikely your video will go viral. Only 1 in 200 videos ever do, according to one musician who posted over 600 daily song videos. It's best to accept that sober fact, but try your hardest anyway. Miles Ludwig, executive producer of *Sesame Street*, explains that its Grover spoof of the Old Spice "The Man Your Man Could Smell Like" commercials went viral because "the online community . . . responded to [the] video." He believes that there's "no

> ### Where to Find Royalty-Free Music
>
> Royalty-free music is music that has been licensed to be used for free. It is the best option for putting music in a video, since it is not copyrighted. There are companies that buy royalty-free music and post it on their websites (with advertisements) for anyone to download. Point your favorite search engine to "royalty free music" for some options.

secret formula for a guaranteed viral hit."[5] Howard Davies-Carr, father of Charlie the finger biter, says, "I would ask why do you want a viral video. I did not set out to do so. I was just lucky or unlucky depending on how you look at it. Set yourself some moral guidelines and keep to them no matter the offers, [which] is probably more difficult than most."[6]

Notes

1. Rennie Dyball, "Is Greyson Chance the Next Justin Bieber (or Lady Gaga)?" May 13, 2010, www.people.com/people/article/0,,20368867,00.html.
2. Greyson Chance, "Bio," 2011, www.greyson-official.com/bio/.
3. Mark Hill, "The 6 Most Insanely Misguided Attempts at Viral Marketing," June 17, 2010, www.cracked.com/article_18569_the-6-most-insanely-misguided-attempts-at-viral-marketing_p1.html.
4. Ted Johnson, "Viacom Loses YouTube Suit," June 23, 2010, www.variety.com/article/VR1118020966?refCatId=4025.
5. Samuel Axon, "The Story behind *Sesame Street*'s Viral Old Spice Spoof," October 12, 2010, http://mashable.com/2010/10/12/sesame-street-old-spice/.
6. William Wei, "Go Viral: Lessons from Hugely Popular YouTube Videos," August 26, 2010, www.businessinsider.com/go-viral-lessons-from-hugely-popular-youtube-videos-2010-8.

ATTUNE TO THE TUNES: MANAGING YOUR MUSIC

....

"Without music, I would not be who I am and having it so easily accessible (especially when bands stream their new material online) opens up entire new worlds of music."
—*Grace, age 16*
"I think online music is awesome, it's convenient and usually free." —*Jack C., age 14*

Music is central to the lives of most people. Many teens consider it easier to concentrate on homework if there is background music playing. Trips are better when everyone can sing along. Just walking home from school is easier with music to set the pace. The Internet makes music much more accessible and easier to acquire. Anyone with an Internet connection can purchase his or her favorite song and load it on a portable music player. It's also easy to find new music, learn about your favorite bands, hear about concerts or CD release news, and connect with other fans.

Two websites are powerhouses in the online music world: for musicians who have made it big, Vevo; for musicians looking to make it big, MySpace.

Vevo.com, created by the major American music companies Universal Music Group and Sony Corp in April 2009, housed approximately 85 percent of all professionally produced American music videos within 6 months of its creation. Vevo continues to corner the market on music videos, giving the only real competition to YouTube, which does not have the business connections and

Music is central to the lives of most people.

Some Stats about Social Networking Sites

- 20 percent of uploads on YouTube are music videos, according to YouTube.
- 13,000,000+ songs are for sale on iTunes, according to Apple.
- The 10,000,000,000th song sold by iTunes was "Guess Things Happen That Way," by Johnny Cash, purchased by Louie Sulcer of Woodstock, Georgia, according to Apple.

therefore focuses on other types of videos.

Meanwhile, MySpace, realizing that it was losing the social network war to Facebook, focused on its core of musicians and its reputation as a place to launch a band without selling out to a big agency. "MySpace has become a destination for music lovers to follow their favorite artists and get the music and video content they crave. Artists in turn are on MySpace because it's still a good distribution channel for their work."[1] But MySpace popularity is declining. It lost over 30 million visitors per month over the course of 2010. A media company and artist Justin Timberlake bought MySpace for a mere $35 million in June 2011, and they plan to develop a new strategy for the site. Other companies are attempting to provide a similar social network for musicians—most notably, Apple's Ping and MTV.

With the success of these two websites come many followers hoping to make it big. Use your favorite search engine to search for *best music social networks* to find suggestions. Also, ask your friends what they use.

Making It Big on MySpace

Rapper Sean Kingston was 17 when a record label found him on MySpace and recognized his talent. He said, "If it wasn't for MySpace, I don't think I'd be where I'm at now."[2] Kingston sent a message to producer J. R. Rotem, inviting him to

What Adults Are Saying

"MySpace still has 110 million users, it's very user-friendly for influencers, and it's a great place to go. A lot of people think the site's dead, which really isn't the case." —Chris DeWolfe, founder of MySpace[3]

check out Kingston's MySpace page—then he sent the same message 5 times a day until Rotem wrote back saying he was taking a look. Kingston's perseverance resulted in an audition that led to a record deal.

Lily Allen, daughter of musician Keith Allen, made a few failed attempts to break into the music business before posting demos on her MySpace account in 2005. "My record company didn't even know what MySpace was," Allen told Pitchfork Media in 2006. "About three weeks after I set it up, my manager called me and he was like, 'I think you ought to set this thing up, it's called MySpace or something,' and I was like, 'Already done it.' It was obvious that something was going on, because there were so many subscribers to the blog and so many people listening to the music—the plays were just going up and up and up."[4]

Ingrid Michaelson, whose music has been featured on a number of popular television shows, was also discovered on MySpace. A talent agency found her music when a friend of Michaelson posted a song on her own MySpace page. Michaelson said that music executives "check out [musicians'] MySpace page first, to see what's up, and then you go check them out and see how they are live—it's like a little preview. It's so easy and it's so accessible to everybody."[5]

Music! For Free! Online! But Is It Okay to Download It?

Many people in the music industry say no; they say that their work is copyrighted and that they make a living from people paying to have access to it. The ability to steal the music from websites cuts into their profit and makes it harder for them

What Teens Are Saying

"I think music online is good and bad. It is a fast way for the consumer to purchase only music they are looking for. It also helps save the environment because it doesn't use resources to create things like CDs. It can be bad for artists though because they do not make as much money because CDs cost more than a single song. Also, people can then spread the music for free by burning or downloading onto other devices and the artist then doesn't make that money." —Adam, age 17

"Usually I buy music on iTunes, but occasionally an artist I like will post a link to a free download to a song or two so I use those as well." —Niki, age 15

to create more music. A recording industry executive told the *Boston Globe*, "It's a little like him standing on street corner and waving everybody over and saying, 'This guy has a table of illegal CDs and you can pick them up for nothing.'"[6] The music industry has filed lawsuits against websites that allow music sharing and even against individuals who used the downloaded files. Each time, the courts have upheld the rights of the musician and music producers, clearly saying that downloading music without purchasing it first is illegal.

Think of it this way—would you steal a CD from a store? Instead of stealing your music online, purchase it legally. There are thousands of places online to buy digital files of your favorite songs, often for less than a dollar per song. Every time you purchase a song instead of stealing it, you are helping the music industry make more music.

Minnesota mom Jammie Thomas-Rasset was charged with downloading and sharing 24 songs illegally from Kazaa.[7] She appealed twice, and each time a jury found her guilty and charged her a different amount: $9,250 per song in 2007, $80,000 per song in 2009, and $62,500 per song in 2010.

So what *is* legal when it comes to sharing music? If you purchased the CD

> ## Napster
>
> Napster was a music-sharing website formed in June 1999 by college students Shawn Fanning and Sean Parker (who went on to help form Facebook). Anonymous users uploaded their digital music to Napster's servers so that other users could download it for free. Musicians found that their songs were being shared on Napster before they were even released to the public, resulting in a number of lawsuits against the company. Use of Napster peaked in February 2001, with 26.4 million users worldwide. It was shut down by court order in July 2001 for copyright infringement but was instrumental in creating a way for music and other files to be shared online.

or digital file, you may make copies of it for your own personal use. That means burning it to a CD or putting it on your MP3 player. You may loan your copy to a friend as long as he or she doesn't copy it. You may play your copy for friends. The point is that you have paid for the right to listen to that music in whatever form you choose, but you have not paid for the right to give a copy to someone else.

The sites you can use to download music and other files illegally are dangerous to use. You may get the song you want, but you will also likely get malware such as viruses, spyware, and unwanted advertising. Teenager Grace says, "I've heard of torrent downloads going wrong, with viruses coming through them, or even this one guy I knew who thought he was downloading the entire Cradle of Filth discography, but instead wasted a huge portion of his download on a fake torrent filled with nursery rhymes!!" Because of the volume of files being uploaded and downloaded via pirate sites, there is no way to determine if the files are dangerous. Therefore, people who want to release a virus will use those unregulated sites first and name the files to make them sound like what you're looking for. When you try to open the file that you downloaded, it will run a program that infects your computer and could automatically infect other computers through your network

What Teens Are Saying

"I like music online; it is very nice to listen to a song in its entirety to see if you like it or not without having to buy it." —Ariel, age 18

"I personally download music. But I guess it's not so uncommon. I used to be against it, but it became increasingly difficult to purchase all the music that I wanted. As music is a huge aspect of my life, I don't always have the money to go out and buy an album when I can download it straight to my computer."
—Grace, age 16

"I don't like the file-sharing websites; I know it's nice to save money, but I'm all for supporting the artists, so I buy all of my music (with the exception of when the artists *themselves* give it out for free)." —Niki, age 15

"I know a high school student who steals small food items from drugstores. Although this disgusts many of my friends, I know that most of those same people condone another type of stealing: illegal downloading."
—Anonymous high school student on YPulse[8]

"I used to use Limewire to download free music, but then it got shut down, so I either watch videos on YouTube, pay to download from iTunes, or rip discs from the library." —Jack C., age 14

or contacts. Often these are brand new malware programs that even the best virus protection program won't be able to catch right away. They could leave your computer completely incapacitated or work quietly behind your other programs to record your passwords, even going so far as to steal your identity! The best way to avoid these problems is to not download the files in the first place. Files purchased legitimately will not have dangerous side effects.

Your computer may be infected by a virus or other malware if it

- Runs slower than usual
- Stops or freezes frequently
- Crashes and needs to be restarted frequently
- Restarts automatically
- Won't allow access to drives
- Pops up random ads, even when you aren't online
- Shows weird menus or dialog boxes
- Stops printing correctly
- Disables the antivirus program
- Suddenly has new icons on the desktop
- Plays strange sounds or music
- Removes files or programs

Another sign is when your friends tell you that they received an e-mail from you that you didn't send, especially if it contained an advertisement.

If your computer is displaying any of these signs, consult your parents for assistance in getting it cleaned. It may require reformatting or taking the computer to a professional!

Finding New (to You) Music

When you're sick of your entire playlist, it's time to seek out some new artists.

Music on Social Networks

Searching for new music on a social networking site is uncommon, but it's likely that your friends have shared their favorite music. Check your friends' profiles for information about favorite bands or for linked music videos. Be sure to put your favorites on your profile for your friends to find.

To link a music video in Facebook, start by finding the video in YouTube or

What Teens Are Saying

"For listening to music online I use either Grooveshark or Pandora if I just want music to be playing, or YouTube if I'm looking for a particular song."
—Averill, age 18

"I *love* Pandora.com. It's a fantastic free radio website, where you can enter an artist, song, or genre and it will create a radio station that contains songs that are similar. A lot of the music I listen to now is from artists I had discovered on Pandora!" —Niki, age 15

another video website. Copy the address of the video, and paste it in the status update box at the top of your profile. You may need to designate that it's a link. Facebook will automatically embed the video, and you can add thoughts of your own before posting.

Music on Music-Sharing Sites

Vevo gives the most popular searches of the day plus What's Hot, which lists the top 10 videos at that time. MySpace Music features playlists and presents top albums and musicians on its main page (www.myspace.com/music).

For something more random, Blip.fm is a music social networking site that focuses on sharing music-related updates. Registration is required but free. Each user, or DJ, creates a playlist of his or her favorite songs that other users can listen to and comment on. Comments about the songs display in a huge status update list. You can search for DJs who have *blipped* (posted about) your favorite artists and then see what else they have deemed worthy of posting.

The Hype Machine

Anthony Volodkin was a sophomore in college when, frustrated with the randomness of radio stations and music magazines, he created the Hype Machine (hypem.com) in 2005. He says, "I kinda felt I hadn't heard anything new that I really enjoyed in a while. But then I discovered MP3 blogs like Stereogum and Music for Robots. I couldn't believe there were people spending their time writing about music, putting up tracks so you could hear them. And I thought, there has to be a way to bring this all together."[9] The site is a list of songs being discussed on any of more than 600 monitored blogs. You can click through to the post or purchase the song via iTunes. The site is visited by a million people per month.

Music on the Internet

Another way to find new music is to listen to Internet radio. Websites such as Pandora.com, the Hype Machine, Last.fm, and Grooveshark.com allow you to create your own station or playlist based on a song, band, or genre of music that you choose. They may include trivia about the bands, but other than sharing playlists or stations with friends, they are not very social.

Billboard, a major music magazine, posts top music lists on its website. Go to billboard.com and click on "Charts" at the very top. You can browse the top 100 songs of the week or choose a music genre or source, such as MySpace Music. You can also choose its Social 50, which lists artists based on how much they are being discussed on various social networking sites.

MTV is also watching musicians on social networking sites with its Music Meter (www.mtvmusicmeter.com/), which rates bands based on quantity of

> ## What Teens Are Saying
>
> "There are so many ways to find music online, which is incredibly convenient, but I still find most of my music from listening to things that my friends play around me, the radio, or other non-Internet ways." —Averill, age 18

comments. Click on an artist to read more about what is being said about him or her, and then choose the *Similar* icon to find other artists. You can also search for an artist directly. You can share the link to your other social networks, but as of 2011, there is no way to reach fans through the MTV site.

Pay attention to what music is used for advertisements or television shows, especially for those brands you like. Advertisers have figured out that they can hire up-and-coming artists for much less money, helping them to rise in fame as well as associate their brand with the new big thing. For example, the band The Fray was featured on the television show *Grey's Anatomy*, and Old Navy used Ingrid Michaelson's music in commercials. When you hear a song that catches your interest, search online for the brand. It's likely the brand's website will tell you the name of the artist.

The Internet is also an excellent source for information about musicians and their music. Wikipedia articles on bands are often written by their biggest fans and can include up-to-the-minute information. Musicians have personal websites and may give concert and release news, lyrics, trivia, photos, and sample music. Searching for the name of the song and the word *lyric* will give you dozens of sites that provide lyrics for every song.

Notes

1. Ben Parr, "Ping Is the Last Nail in the Coffin for MySpace," September 1, 2010, http://mashable.com/2010/09/01/ping-myspace/.

2. MySpace, "Sean Kingston Gets Discovered on MySpace," June 29, 2007, www.myspace.com/video/vid/11793450.

3. Jim Squires, "Former CEO DeWolfe Discusses Making MySpace Relevant Again," June 21, 2010, www.gamezebo.com/news/2010/07/21/former-ceo-dewolfe-discusses-making-myspace-relevant-again.

4. Scott Plagenoef, "Lily Allen," November 6, 2006, http://pitchfork.com/features/interviews/6476-lily-allen/.

5. Talk of the Nation, "The Making of Musicians on MySpace," May 21, 2007, www.npr.org/templates/story/story.php?storyId=10300691.

6. W. David Gardner, "Pirate Bay's '$675,000 Mixtape' Irks RIAA," *InformationWeek*, September 4, 2009.

7. "$1.8m for Net Piracy," *New Zealand Herald*, November 6, 2010: 8.

8. Anonymous, "Confessions of a Teenage Internet Pirate," May 24, 2011, www.ypulse.com/confessions-of-a-teenage-Internet-pirate.

9. John Heilemann, "Capturing the Buzz," March 15, 2007, http://money.cnn.com/magazines/business2/business2_archive/2006/10/01/8387122/index.htm.

SAY CHEESE! MANAGE YOUR PHOTOS

....

"I post photos on Facebook, just to document the school year, vacations, marching band season, things like that." —Niki, age 15

A camera in every pocket means that there are billions of photos to upload, edit, comment on, and admire. This chapter focuses on how to handle your photos, plus where to find great photos taken by others.

Which site you use to display your photos is a personal choice. Ask your friends what they prefer because using the same site as everyone you care about will make it easier for all your friends to see and comment on your photos. Also, they can help you if you get stuck using the site.

Photos on Social Networks

All major social networking sites have the ability to display photos. Look for the *Photo* tab or link toward the top of your main page to find the place to upload photos.

It is a good idea to create folders to keep your photos organized and to make it easy for your friends to browse to the event that they want to see. Name your album something that makes sense to other people—"Party at Aiden's" or "4th of July weekend with Helena and Caleb"—and include a date or at least the year.

Say cheese!

What Teens Are Saying

"I don't see the use and/or reason for a service that only shares photos such as Flickr. I see using Facebook and bit URL services such as Twitpic with Twitter much more useful. But Picasa is very valuable because it helps organize [my photos] on my computer." —Jack S., age 17

"Sometimes I download photos for projects, to use as screensavers, or to create photo collages for my school binders, but I don't really do much with photos online." —Ariel, age 18

Most sites allow you to tag a friend in your photos. When you turn on tagging, you can click on a person's face in the photo and label him or her. It connects the photo to that person's profile and notifies him or her that you have posted a photo. Other people who look at your friend's profile will also see your photo.

When you create an album, you can set who can see that album. You can make them completely private, allow only your friends to view the photos, or permit anyone access. Some sites have extra options, such as giving access to friends of your friends. Think about the photos that you are posting when setting this option, and limit access to what should be private. Only use the *Everyone* setting if every photo in the folder does not contain people.

Find your friends' photos by going to their profiles. The *Photo* tab or link should be at the top of the page. You can comment and tag your friends' photos by clicking on them. You can also share other people's photos, which posts them on your profile and allows you to make a comment about them.

Photos on Photo-Sharing Sites

There are sites intended just for sharing photos that you can link to from your profile. The most frequently used site is Flickr.com, but many people prefer

How Embarrassing!

Never post photos that could be embarrassing for you or anyone else. Remember that anyone can download your photos (usually by right clicking on the photo and choosing *Save image as*) and do whatever they want with them. That includes editing and reposting them! It is best to just never put up the photos that are embarrassing or could be misused easily. Your friends would prefer that you only post attractive photos of them anyway!

If a friend posts a picture of you that you find embarrassing or inappropriate, talk to him or her about it. If you explain why, that person will probably take the photo down. At the very least, you can choose to remove a tag of yourself from any photo.

Photobucket.com or ImageShack.us. All of these sites require you to register and create a log-in but do not require you to pay. Play around with all of them until you decide which one works best for you—or ask your friends what they use.

After you have registered, you'll start by uploading the photos you want to store on the site. Find the *Upload* button at the top of your main profile page; the web designers make it fairly obvious, since it's the main point of the site. It allows you to choose photos from your computer to upload. Then you can organize your photos in folders; add tags, titles, and descriptions; and share your photos on other sites or via e-mail. Most photo sites allow you to have friends and comment on other peoples' photos.

These sites also let you do fun things that aren't easily available in bigger social networks. For instance, *geotagging* is available in Facebook, but there is no real way to search by those tags. Geotagging is when you identify that a photo was taken in a certain spot, sometimes narrowing it down to a specific place on a satellite map.

What Teens Are Saying

"The only photos I use are Facebook. That is just to share memories with friends." —Adam, age 17

"With tagging it's even really easy to find the photo you're looking for because you don't have to worry about remembering who uploaded a certain photo." —Averill, age 18

"Don't really use anything other than Facebook to house my pictures. Then again, I don't take many pictures." —Bow, age 20

"I don't use Flickr since Facebook's got everything." —Priyanka, age 15

On sites such as Flickr, you can choose a location, and see what photos have been taken there. Try looking up your hometown!

Altering Your Photos

There are many things you can do with a photo to change it—from simple things such as cropping and fixing red eye to complex alterations and collages. Most photo-sharing sites give you the option of editing your photos.

Also, there are free programs you can use online or download that will give you even more editing power. For instance, Picasa (http://picasa.google.com/) is a downloadable photo organizer and editor that links to Google's photo-sharing site of the same name. Other popular editors are Paint.NET (www.getpaint.net) and Photoscape (www.photoscape.org). Flickr uses a photo-editing program called Picnik, which opens up right in your Flickr account.

Size Limits

Some photos are too large to be uploaded to your favorite site. Facebook limits photos at 15 MB, Flickr at 10 MB, and Photobucket only 5 MB. If you have a really good camera, your photos may be larger than these limits. Most photo-editing programs allow you to compress photos, which will reduce the size but can make the picture grainy. To find out how, type "Compress" into the help search.

The Basics

Any picture could improve with some cropping. The crop tool allows you to draw a square on your photo to show what portion you want to keep. Use this tool to focus on the interesting part of the photo, especially when the photo has a lot of unnecessary blank space.

Fixing red eye is a tool that allows you to remove the red glow from a person's eye. When it is turned on, click on the red part of an eye, and it will mask the red with another color. Some editors have other options that allow you to cover over a pimple, smooth out a wrinkle, or remove red eye on a pet.

Resizing allows you to choose what size the photo will be. This is important if the photo is displaying much too large or too small on the website. Make sure to click the *Keep proportions* option because that will make your photo stay the same shape as you resize it.

When your photo is sideways, use the rotate tool to turn it upright. Some editors also have a straighten tool, which allows you to nudge a photo to make it appear level. This is useful when you tilted the camera a bit while taking the photo or if the photo was scanned and wasn't perfectly square in the scanner. You can

Some Stats about Flickr, According to Flickr

- 5,000,000,000th photo archived on Flickr was uploaded on September 19, 2010.
- 3,000 photos uploaded every minute on Flickr in 2010.

also use the rotate and straighten tools to make a photo look off-kilter for effect or to turn it backward.

What about a photo that is too dark or overexposed? Photo editors have contrast and brightness tools for this problem. Contrast adjusts the amount of black in the picture, while brightness adjusts the amount of white. You will probably like the effect more if you use both settings together. Turning up the brightness will make the photo lighter, but then turning up the contrast makes the shadows darker, and the overall look is improved.

You can also adjust the colors of a photo using the color saturation tool. Saturation indicates how much color is in the picture, so zero color would be black

What Teens Are Saying

"Despite Flickr's attractive features and teens craving for photos (especially those featuring themselves with their friends or family members), it's quite rare to see teens on the Yahoo subsidiary. Why? Well, in addition to being a popular website for users to share personal photographs, the service is widely used by bloggers and professional photographers as a photo repository. What teens want or need is just a simple service that allows them to upload and share personal photos with their fellow friends. That's all. However, Flickr is way too complicated for them. Facebook is definitely the most suitable alternative."

—Xavier, age 16, on TechXav[1]

> ### Where It All Began: Flickr
>
> The creation of Flickr is an example of how projects never quite go how you expect. Ludicorp, the Canadian company that launched Flickr in 2004, originally planned to create an online game. Caterina Fake, cofounder of Ludicorp, realized that the tool to share photos in the game was more fun than the game itself. Fake told *USA Today*: "Had we sat down and said, 'Let's start a photo application,' we would have failed, we would have done all this research and done all the wrong things."[2]

and white. Temperature indicates how red or blue the picture is. Again, you will get the best effect if you use both tools together.

If your photos are a bit blurry (which seems to happen way too often!), you can make them clear with the sharpen tool. Don't overdo it—too much sharpening can pixilate the photo and make it look grainy.

Most editors have an autofix that will change all of these things the way that the program thinks is best. While you may disagree and want to do the changes your own way, it's at least worth a look to see if the autofix does a photo good. If not, you can always undo it.

Fun Stuff

Now that you've made your photos look good, it's time to make them look interesting! Remixed photos are often called *photoshopped* or just *'shopped* after the program Photoshop. You don't actually need Photoshop to "shop" your own photos (although it is a really good program if you have access to it). Most photo-editing programs and photo-sharing sites have the ability to do many fun things with your photos. For example, Photobucket has quite a few fun effects, including the ability to make your photo look like a cartoon, a painting, a neon sign, a

---

What Teens Are Saying

"I use Facebook to upload pictures because then all my peers and family can see what I have been up to. I use http://pixlr.com/editor/ to edit photos because it is free and pretty good to edit pictures." —Daniel, age 17

"If used wisely, photos can be a nice networking tool, almost like making a scrapbook online! Other photo-related websites I use include Picnik, which is an editing site to add cool effects to photos, and flickr, which I browse for interesting photos to edit." —Niki, age 15

---

blueprint, a pixilation, a rubber stamp, or a sketch. You can make the photo look old, out of focus, or even a negative.

Keep in mind, though, that this is a face out in the world: be nice about the modifications you make. This is another time when something embarrassing or inappropriate can turn out bad. Before you post, always stop to think about what your joke might mean to the people it targets!

Photobucket (and many other photo sites) gives you tools to decorate photos. You can add captions, thought/speech bubbles, and graphical stickers; erase portions; and even draw on the photo with a pencil or paintbrush. You can also add animated captions and graphics for photos that you are posting online.

Photobucket also includes a cutout feature, which allows you to erase portions of a photo and then can layer the photo with another photo.

For all these sites, there is a *Help* button if you get stuck or can't figure out how to make something work. If that fails, consult a friend for help.

The Ultimate in Photo Decorating: Lolcats

A lolcat is an image (not always of a cat) combined with a humorous caption usually written in grammatically incorrect English meant to parody the poor grammar

---

What Teens Are Saying

"Lots of bad photos get put on there that will never go away." —Ariel, age 18

"When [photos] are online, they always stay online. I have added some pictures of myself on one of my websites and now they are on Google pictures when you type in my name." —Daniel, age 17

"I think that good photos are excellent, but bad photos will rot your brain and mess you up in the future." —Jake, age 13

---

sometimes used on the Internet. The name lolcat was first used in 2005, but it wasn't until the launch of I Can Has Cheezburger? (http://icanhascheezburger .com/) that lolcats became popular.

Some common lolspeak (the language of lolcats) terms:

Hai = hi

RLY? = Oh, really?

NO WA! = No way!

Moar = more

Plz = please

Nom = to eat

Ur = your

Meh = me

Teh = the

Goggie = dog

Kiteh = kitten

Kthxbi = Okay, thanks, bye!

If you find it difficult to understand lolspeak, try this dictionary: http:// speaklolspeak.com/.

I Can Has Cheezburger has a LOL Builder that you can use to create your own lolcats quickly and easily. Just upload your photo, give it a caption, and save it.

Finding Photos

> **! DeviantART.com**
>
> Looking for a place to post your own artwork? The website deviantART.com provides a place for artists of all types to post their creative endeavors to share with the world. It also allows you to search the site for pictures.

Picture this: you need a photo of Abe Lincoln for a homework assignment. Or you really need to find a picture of a bulldog because your best friend hates bulldogs and you want to put one in a photo collage you're making for her. Or you're looking for a nice picture to use as your desktop. Where do you find that photo?

On Social Networks

Depending on the security of your favorite social networking site, you may or may not be able to search for photos. This is not the best place to find a photo unless you know that your friend posted it there. You can always see the photos that your friends have made public or at least accessible to friends, but the best way to find them is to go to a friend's page and look at the photos one by one.

On Photo-Sharing Sites

All photo-sharing sites have some way to search the public photos on the site, with some even allowing voting by users to decide the best picture of the day. Look for links to find stuff or explore—it should be at the top of the website.

Photo-sharing sites may have contests that you can vote on—and what better way to find the coolest photos than in a contest? On Photobucket, click on *Contests* under *Find Stuff* to see what contests are going on right now. You can submit your own photo and vote on other peoples' entries.

Additionally, some photo-sharing sites post only noncopyrighted photos. Try wikimedia.com or search for *free photos*. Sometimes these sites are more difficult to use or may not include the exact photo that you need, but they are safer to use. Averill suggests, "A great place to find photos was FlikrCC. It's a collection of photos that the photographers have released the rights to, so you can use them, and they are usually all really well shot, well edited, and all around good photos."

On the Internet

Search engines such as Yahoo and AltaVista can look for images too. Google's image search allows you to limit in various ways—for example, clip art or a line drawing instead of a photograph or a photo that includes a face. It also can limit the search to pictures with a certain color: if you want a picture of clouds but need them to be dark and gray, you can set the color limit and get only gray clouds.

One of the drawbacks of doing an image search in any search engine is that the pictures that come up may not match your terms. It is searching for your keywords in the captions and nearby text, and if the website creator has labeled something in a weird way, you may get weird results. As with any Internet search, try different terms to be creative.

Using the Photos You Find

Now that you've found a photo for your project, you should consider whether it is okay for you to use it. Photos are protected by copyright just like a book or movie, even those you find online. However, there is a part of the copyright law called *fair use*, which says that it is legal for you to use a small portion of copyrighted material for certain reasons. One reason to use someone else's work is for educational purposes, which means that it is okay to use a single photograph

Placing Your Picture in a Document

Once you have your picture, you need to place it in your assignment. Photos in word-processing programs such as Microsoft Word have properties that you can adjust. If you are struggling to get your photo to line up in just the right way, right click on it and choose *Format Picture*. Under the *Layout* tab, you have some options regarding how text wraps around your picture:

In line with text: no text wrap around the picture, good for when you want the picture to go between paragraphs.

Square and tight: wraps the text around the picture and allows you to put it wherever you want on the page. Shift it around to get the text to wrap around it correctly.

Behind text: the picture is behind the text, good for watermarks and background pictures.

In front of text: the picture goes over the text.

Hint: if you are printing a bunch of pictures on a single page, put them all in *Behind text* layout because then you can arrange them without everything moving around as you do it.

as long as you cite your source in your assignment. Consult your teachers on what they expect.

When in doubt, ask for permission first. If there is contact information on the web page that you want to use, it's easy enough to send a quick e-mail to the photographer explaining why you would like to use the picture. Most of the time, the owners will be happy to let you. Be sure to respect their wishes if they say no or ask you to give them credit in a certain way.

Also consider how your photos might be used after you post them online. Flickr asks you to choose how your uploaded photographs will be covered under Creative

Commons license, so you should understand what limitations you are placing on your uploads when you make that choice. Plenty of people are searching photo-sharing sites for photographs that they can use for their own needs—just as you would in searching for a school assignment—but you may not approve of the way that they use your property.

For example, Virgin Mobile Pty Ltd, an Australian cell phone company, used a photo from Flickr in an ad campaign that humiliated Alison Chang, the girl pictured, according to the lawsuit that her family brought against the company in 2007. The person who posted the photo gave it the Creative Commons copyright license that allows reuse of the photo as long as credit is given. The ad does have the photographer's Flickr site address in the fine print. Virgin Mobile released a statement saying that it used the photo lawfully: "The images have been featured within the positive spirit of the Creative Commons Agreement, a legal framework voluntarily chosen by the photographers. It allows for their photographs to be used for a variety of purposes, including commercial activities."

A representative of Virgin Mobile also said, "This was never based on exploiting the Flickr community, quite the opposite—we felt it would be a great idea to use the creative commons license to champion the world of Flickr."[3] In the end, Virgin Mobile won the case because, in part, the company had followed the license put on the photo.

Keep this ad campaign in mind when you decide how to copyright your own photos, especially those picturing your friends and family.

Notes

1. Xavier Lur, "5 Social Websites That Are Unpopular amongst Teens," March 16, 2010, www.techxav.com/2010/03/16/5-social-websites-that-are-unpopular-amongst-teens/.
2. Jefferson Graham, "Flickr of Idea on a Gaming Project Led to Photo Website," *USA Today*, February 27, 2006, www.usatoday.com/tech/products/2006-02-27-flickr_x.htm.
3. "Teen Finds Her Flickr Image on Bus Stop Ad," February 11, 2009, www.cbsnews.com/stories/2007/09/24/tech/main3290986.shtml?source=RSSattr= SciTech_3290986.

LOVE THEM, MAY AS WELL FOLLOW THEM: CELEBRITIES

"Sometimes it is interesting to learn more personal information about them."
—Ariel, age 18

Actors, musicians, athletes, political figures—they're online too! The Internet has given celebrities a safe way to interact with their fans; therefore, it is possible for you to keep up with your favorite stars and heroes. Many famous people maintain a social presence, and you can get to know them.

It's not all good, though. Some stars forget their audience and say things online that they later regret (just like us!). They have to learn that the Internet is permanent and that they need to protect their privacy just like you. Unfortunately, some celebrities have had bad experiences with fans who have overstepped the boundaries of polite social networking. There is a fine line between following and stalking, and you don't want to be the stalker!

Finding Famous People Online

If your celebrity wants to be found, it really is as easy as searching for the person's name in a search engine or in the people search on a social networking site. Keep in mind that many celebrity social networking profiles are not run by the actual

What Teens Are Saying

"I never really felt the need to follow anyone, or idolize them really in any way. I can, however, see the appeal. I am sure that it is fun to feel connected with someone who you've listened to or seen on the big screen or something, and I'm sure that it would even be more thrilling to have them respond to one of your e-mails or comments or something. After all, a lot of teenagers see these celebrities as the ideal sort of person and therefore look up to them and try to model themselves after them (and even I have to say that I am somewhat influenced by what my favorite singers, actors and actresses have to say)."
—Jade, age 18

"I wouldn't follow famous people too closely, because when they do something that ruins their life, you are devastated. [I think] the responses are from people that are paid to respond, and they are not the real thing." —Jake, age 13

Famous people have online lives too.

"I seriously doubt it's actually them on there anyway." —Ava, age 16

"I have liked pages of famous people on Facebook, but never do anything past that." —Adam, age 17

"I dislike anyone famous; they think that they are the best. And I hate it how when a celebrity or anyone famous does something wrong they can get off with it." —Daniel, age 17

"I don't 'follow' anyone. I am interested in Steven Tyler because I think he's cool, occasionally I look at his bio on imdb.com." —Jack C., age 14

"Following celebrities is just absurd. If you're shallow enough to do that, then social networking has nothing to do with your deteriorating spelling and grammar." —Ava, age 16

"When you are famous you probably get tons of notifications and other things which I think is really hectic. I just think that it's waste of time interacting with celebrities. They wouldn't know you, it's just virtual." —Priyanka, age 15

celebrity; some of them have publicists that keep them up-to-date. In many cases, the person who is actually writing the content will say so, but sometimes he or she doesn't.

The hardest part is telling which of the profiles that come up in a search is the real celebrity's site. Here are some tips:

- Look for the profile that has thousands of followers or friends, significantly more than any other profile.
- Don't trust profile names that are misspelled. Even celebrities can spell their own names! Also, a slightly misspelled name is one way that an impostor will get around rules against putting up fake profiles.

Some Stats about the Obama Social Media Campaign, According to the *Washington Post*

- 5,000,000 Barack Obama supporters on over 15 networks
- 24,500,000 Barack Obama channel views on YouTube as of 2011
- $6,500,000 contributed by 3 million online donors to the 2008 Obama campaign. $6,000,000 of it was collected at less than $100 per donation.

- Be careful about trusting profiles that say they are "the real one" or something similar. The true celebrity may not bother with such assertions.
- Check details on the profile—are they accurate?
- Are there personal pictures mixed in with official ones? Most celebrities include photos of themselves at family gatherings or behind the scenes at work. If the personal photo is taken from across the street, that's probably not the right profile.
- If they are available online all the time, it's likely not them, since most celebrities don't have time to hang out online constantly.
- If they have family members in their friends list, check those people to see if they have any other famous people friended. If not, it's likely that this is the true celebrity profile. A celebrity's brother probably wouldn't friend too many other celebrities.

Not Finding Your Celebrity?

When you've searched in all the usual places and you just haven't found that famous person, consider that the person isn't online. Some celebrities choose not to be a part of the social networking world. It's best to respect their privacy.

THE_REAL_SHAQ[1]

There was a lot of speculation about who was the real Shaquille O'Neal on Twitter in 2008. One Twitter user, Bryant Blount (Twitter name: lord_b), decided to follow Shaq and was surprised when Shaq followed him back. He tweeted, "shaq has requested to follow me . . . boy is he gonna be disappointed." Blount was even more surprised when Shaq asked for his phone number and then called him!

Kathleen Hessert, Shaq's online marketing manager, said, "Shaq is a joyful person and a riot to be around. He not only gets attention but actually attracts people—he's magnetic and genuine. That's why I recommended that he twitter."

- Check the celebrity's links and notes. If they're advertisements, it's not real.

It's unlikely that celebrities would be interested in chatting freely with the general public, and they certainly wouldn't tell you their mundane troubles or ask you out. Trust your instincts.

You may have better luck going to the famous person's Wikipedia article or official website, which is often sponsored by the company that pays him or her (e.g., a movie production company or a sports team). Most famous-people websites will give a link to their official pages on social networking sites. If they have a contact option, you can ask for the link. You can also use celebrity search websites to get links. Direct your favorite search engine to *finding celebrities online* to get a list. Compare a couple of them to make sure that the link you've found is the best one.

Once you've found a celebrity you are sure is the real deal, look through his or her friends list. Celebrities do have personal friends who are celebrities and thus may be more likely to have another celebrity's actual profile linked.

Top Celebrities

The following is a list of the top celebrities worldwide on social networks as of July 26, 2011, according to Famecount.com and based on the number of fans at Facebook, followers on Twitter, and subscriptions on YouTube:

1. Lady Gaga
2. Justin Bieber
3. Rihanna
4. Eminem
5. Shakira
6. Katy Perry
7. Barack Obama
8. Taylor Swift
9. Michael Jackson
10. Selena Gomez

Being a Good Follower

Celebrities are people too! They have lives outside their job of being famous. Always keep that in mind when you're interacting with them on their social networking sites.

Common blunders that fans make are to monopolize the celebrity's attention, to flatter one excessively, to disrespect his or her privacy, or to be pushy. Also, don't be overly familiar; you may feel that you know celebrities because you follow them online or listen to their music every day, but you are a complete stranger to them. Maintain a polite and respectful demeanor at all times. A short, well-written, genuine compliment is always best.

When following actors and actresses, separate the person from his or her role.

Never call an actor by his character name or ask her to perform something that her character is famous for. Don't blame the actor for the actions of the character. Instead, give a heartfelt opinion of the person's acting skill or congratulations for an achievement.

A good rule of thumb is to think about how you would want to be treated in the celebrity's shoes. That will guide you in how you should behave as well as what you expect from the celebrity in return. Remember that celebrities have very busy lives keeping up whatever has made them famous. As much as they might want to be friends with their fans, they often can't. Consider it a huge compliment if they reply to you in any way, and don't expect more than that.

Meeting a celebrity, even online, can be quite an exciting event. Don't lose yourself in the excitement and forget to be respectful!

> **What Teens Are Saying**
>
> "Some [celebrities] take it way too far. Some things are just too personal and should be left so, like pictures of them with their family or out on dates. . . . [They] open themselves up to that kind of exposure willingly."
> —Ariel, age 18

Finding Celebrity Gossip

There are social networking sites for fans that will tell you about the celebrity. These are news sites, forums, or wikis dedicated to that person or company. These sites should come up in a general search engine search, in the search on your favorite wiki website, or in searches for "celebrity news" to get general aggregators. Also, check the celebrity's Wikipedia page to get links to other sources.

Teen Celebrity Entrepreneurs

Miley Cyrus was a Disney star and, therefore, everywhere she could be, but it was her skill on the Internet that really made her popular. Mitchell Gossett, her agent

> **Phrase Searching**
>
> If you are having trouble finding your celebrity in an Internet search, try putting quotes around his or her name. This will tell the search engine to search for those words together as a phrase instead of as separate words—for example, "Shaquille O'Neal."

at the time, says that it was her personal knowledge of viral marketing that made her a success. He said, "Miley had this machine behind her, but she also knew how to use the Internet to generate the undercurrent for her extraordinary rise."[2]

Justin Bieber got his start on YouTube when his mother posted videos of him singing. The videos were accidentally found by a music agent looking for another singer. Bieber was 14 when he signed with a major record label. "The harder you work, the more successful you can be," he said. "This is just the beginning for me."[3]

Lucas Cruikshank was 13 when he created the squeaky-voiced Fred Figglehorn, a 6-year-old with a temper and family issues, and started filming videos. Cruikshank got the idea for Fred when he was reading blogs and found them trivial: "[Blog writers] complain the whole entire day and think everyone's so interested in it. I expected [Fred] to be big, but definitely not this big."[4] In April 2009, Fred's YouTube channel hit 1 million subscribers, making Cruikshank the first person to reach that number. Nickelodeon hopes to help Fred move to creating more professional videos, starting with a movie released in 2010. As of 2011, Cruikshank's videos of Fred on YouTube have been viewed over 400,000,000 times.

Not all teen celebrities are celebrated online. Jade comments, "I was always told that people who 'made it' were just as talented as many other people, the only difference between them and everybody else was that they had connections or simply got lucky." Child actor Jaden Smith, son of actor Will Smith, has met resentment and hate on forums and websites. "Let's start with the indisputable fact that Smith got to be in the position he's in because his father is the biggest movie star on the planet," says *Entertainment Weekly* film critic

Owen Gleiberman. He continues, "Should we hate every young actor or musician who ever got placed on the map of fame because of his or her parents?"[5] It appears that the reason why Smith is bashed so much is an appearance of favoritism, since he comes across as cocky about being cast in major movies.

How to Be the Celebrity

Just as celebrities can reach their fans because of the Internet, now everyone has access to a global audience, making it easier than ever to become famous. How would you go about getting to be as famous as Fred?

For starters, you need to have something unique to display online. It could be an extraordinary skill or unusual viewpoint or something only you do. It needs to be more than a gimmick such as a squeaky voice, but you can use a trick to make your special something interesting to a wide variety of people. The content is the most important part of making yourself famous.

Then you have to find a way to record your special something in a way that accentuates the uniqueness and makes it interesting. Many Internet stars are found through videos, but yours may come across better in photography, a podcast, a blog, or a game. Create a teaser with as much polish and professionalism as you can, and then do follow-up recordings to continue holding interest. If possible, keep your product short: 2 minutes is a good cutoff.

Then post it everywhere! Viral content is judged based on the number of times it is viewed, which is directly affected by the number of times it is shared. How often it is shared depends entirely on how much work you put into advertising. Put it on every social media site you can find, and publish links to it from every forum, blog, or website you have access to. Post it with different titles and blurbs so that it catches a variety of search terms. Use free promotional tools, such as Digg and Google AdSense, and consider paid advertising on major sites like Facebook. Finally, tell everyone you know about it, out in the real world. Talk it up at parties, and pitch it as an article for the local newspaper or radio shows. If you're really serious, find an agent! The point is to get it out there to literally everywhere you can and then hope it will spread.

Be careful to be honest about who you are throughout your advertising effort. Don't spam sources that would be uninterested in your product; instead, find those forums and sites that would be interested. Don't add fake comments to your own post or create fake accounts. People don't like to be deceived, and you don't want to be known as that guy or girl who lied.

And after you do all of this, cross your fingers. There is no set way to get content to go viral and become popular. It starts with lots of people talking about the content and sharing it with their friends, but the step between people you know and being an Internet sensation is invisible and nearly impossible to find. If the first time doesn't work, try again!

Notes

1. Adam Ostrow, "How a Tweet Led to a Phone Call from Shaq," November 21, 2008, http://mashable.com/2008/11/21/shaq-twitter/.
2. Maureen Farrell, "The Most Successful Teen Celebrity Entrepreneurs," June 11, 2010, www.forbes.com/2010/06/11/teen-celebrities-brand-building-entrepreneurs-miley-cyrus-justin-bieber.html.
3. Jan Hoffman, "Justin Bieber Is Living the Dream," *New York Times*, December 31, 2009, www.nytimes.com/2010/01/03/fashion/03bieber.html.
4. CNN.com, "American Morning," July 11, 2008, http://edition.cnn.com/TRANSCRIPTS/0807/11/ltm.02.html.
5. Owen Gleiberman, "Why the Hatred for Jaden Smith? It's the Ugly Underside of Fan Worship," June 18, 2010, http://insidemovies.ew.com/2010/06/18/why-the-hatred-for-jaden-smith/.

GET THOSE A'S: DOING SCHOOL

"I just Google everything. When I don't get it I just Google it." —Priyanka, age 15

Our world is moving more and more online, and many aspects of our culture are taking advantage of social media websites to make life better and easier. Your school probably has a website where you can contact your teachers, research for homework assignments, or see what the cafeteria is serving for lunch tomorrow. Your parents can likely track your performance and attendance through a website

Use social media tools to excel in school.

What Teens Are Saying

"Technology has been bad for me as a student but good for me as a learner. . . . I can always apply myself and be more motivated to learn something when . . . I'm choosing my own curriculum. . . . You have so much information. . . . It can serve as a distraction from things you have to do, like, in my case, schoolwork. . . . After spending three hours looking up cameras or video editing or something like that, I feel like I've accomplished more for myself than sitting down to write an essay." —Vishal, high school student, in the *New York Times*[1]

"Because many teens are convinced that socializing online is more important than being on top of their studies, too many are unaware of current events or how to solve simple math problems. Most of the students I know want to learn and do well. But it is difficult for them to do so with all of the distractions social networking sites have to offer." —Alycia, high school student, in *The Record*[2]

"My school has us join Podium and Moodle, but we only use them once or twice a year for group projects, and when we do the projects we feel more like the teachers wanted to use a new format to teach in than they are actually better projects because they had this online component. I would have rather had an in class discussion on the book, that way you could actually have a flowing conversation that everyone could keep up with than do an online forum and either have to wait a day and a half for a reply or log on to find that you missed a huge argument that you would have had points to contribute if only you were online at 1:43 AM the night before." —Averill, age 18

that your teachers keep updated. Social media sites also make it easier to contact your classmates outside of school, do group assignments, and create higher-level products.

These resources are available in the *cloud*, a technical term for a software program that is run entirely on the Internet rather than downloaded to your computer.

What Teens Are Saying

"If you have a question on homework you post it as a status. If someone reads your status and can help they will comment on your status." —Adam, age 17

"There's always someone in your class online if you need to ask a more specialized question." —Averill, age 18

"I like to e-mail my peers if I am stuck on what to do or mostly I use Facebook to ask my peers what we need to do or what they are doing." —Daniel, age 17

"If I'm stumped on homework, I'll usually text or IM a friend to ask what they think or what they did to finish it. Also, if I'm searching for information online and can't find it, I'll go to AskColorado, that site where you can IM a librarian and they help find info." —Niki, age 15

Most websites that you use are part of the cloud because you create a product on the website (such as a status update, blog entry, or homework document) and then save it on that website. Because the data are saved online, you can access them from any computer; you can also give multiple people access to it as you see fit, thus allowing classmates and your teachers to be involved.

Those teachers who didn't grow up with the same social tools as your generation may find it difficult to incorporate them into their classrooms; they may not even realize they're not doing it. One study, Project Tomorrow's Speak Up 2010, found that 74 percent of high school teachers and 72 percent of principals felt that their school was using technology to enhance classroom learning, but only 47 percent of their students agreed. The study also found that 53 percent of middle school and high school students felt that inability to use their phones or music players in school was an obstacle, and 71 percent of high school students felt that digital content would be more useful if the school didn't filter it.

Places to Get Online Homework Help *Right Now*

That math problem is more than what your parents understand, so where do you turn for help at 9 PM on a school night?

- Check to see if your friends are online, especially if they have the same assignment.
- Check to see if your teacher is online.
- Visit your school library's website for additional resources.
- Visit your public library's website for additional resources.
- Your public or school library may also offer an online tutor.

This chapter addresses some resources that you can use for school (and personal) projects, whether your teachers are involved or not.

Using Social Networks for School Assignments

Friending your classmates gives you an after-hours line of communication with them. Create a group page so all members can see posts; use the forum to discuss the project; schedule study groups as events; or upload photos and files of your progress. You can also use the chat feature to discuss the assignment, although often only two people can be involved.

Using a site such as Facebook for this kind of group work requires that all members have an account, so consider that when determining where to meet electronically. You may also find that exchanging e-mails or IM log-ins is helpful. Be sure to talk about what websites would be most useful for the group at your very first meeting.

> ## What Teens Are Saying
>
> "For group projects, I recommend setting up a time to meet in person. In person a person's thoughts and emotions are truly exposed so it's easier to make everyone feel like they're having input into the project." —Bow, age 20
>
> "Text is also used to coordinate projects if there is a time constraint. That allows faster collaboration between two people than either Facebook or e-mail."
> —Adam, age 17

Using Your School's Tools

Consider what your school website offers that could be useful for you. Your school may have a Facebook page that you can follow to see news and updates. Your teachers may also use a wiki or Ning to post lecture notes, helpful resources, or homework assignments. (See chapter 5 for more information about wikis and Ning.)

Your school may also offer an online collaboration tool, such as Blackboard or Moodle. These are closed social networking sites available only to your teachers and classmates. They can provide space for forums, file upload, group chat rooms, group documents, and more. If you are having a problem with a school-provided tool, ask your teacher for assistance.

Many schools are requiring students to have log-ins to a certain social network, such as Google's Apps for Education or Microsoft's Live@edu, so students can work together through the network. Some teachers are even allowing files and projects saved within Google Docs to be the final product, since the teachers can also access the work and can even sometimes see who did what portions.

Simple Ways That You Can Use Your Cell Phone to Help with Your Schoolwork

- Record assignment due dates and tests in your calendar.
- Photograph the assignment written on the board.
- Set up homework reminders via texting services.
- Use a task organizer app to keep track of homework assignments and when to work on what.
- Set your alarm to remind you to do homework.
- Use a notes app to take notes in class or make a plan for a project.
- Use the calculator.
- Use the camera or video and audio recorders when doing multimedia projects.
- Text ideas and facts to a classmate, giving you both a written record.
- Use the Internet browser to look up facts needed for a project.
- Struggling with math or vocabulary? Search for an app on the topic!
- Download an e-book or audiobook of required reading titles.
- Audio record a lecture (ask the teacher's permission first), and replay it while going over your notes.

Working in an Online Group

It can be frustrating to work in an online group, especially if the members don't have opportunities to meet in person. When your group is together in real life, there is a lot of body language to read, and it's easy for the conversation to go off topic in a way that keeps everyone interested and friendly. Online, it can be one person sending an e-mail that the others don't know how to respond to and *poof!*—no communication. It also can be difficult when everyone checks e-mail at different times, and decisions can't just get made. Keep these problems in mind when you're working in an online group. There are some ways to make the experience easier.

When working with a group online, establish a communication plan. Find a tool that is available to all members of the group, and plan on times to meet using that tool. Start by asking which social media sites everyone uses. This topic can also be a good conversation starter, especially if you don't know the other group members. Finding out about the other members will help you bond as a group, so ask them about their interests and personal lives. Work together to figure out one another's strengths and how to apply them to the project you're doing together. Then create a list of things that need to happen, and give a deadline for each. Everyone in the group can work together to assign each piece to the person with the most skills for that task. It is also important to work together toward a goal, so make sure that everyone understands how his or her piece will contribute to the final project.

One role in an online group could be that of facilitator. This person keeps track of all the deadlines and pieces, checking in with each group member on his or her individual progress. Depending on the group, this could be an informal position or a role that is equal in work to the others. Talk about your expectations for the group, and establish this role with someone whom the whole group respects and is willing to work with.

If you have a member of your group who is not doing her or his share, talk to your teacher about the issue. He or she may have advice on how to help that person do the work. If you need to deal with it alone, consider exactly what the problem is and confront the person. It is best to concentrate on the problem rather than the person. If necessary, consider working with the rest of the group to cover the portion that is not being done, and be sure to explain to your teacher what happened.

While working in a group online can be a challenge, it can also be very rewarding. Using an online tool to discuss and plan a project as a group can give even the quietest student the opportunity to include an opinion. You may be surprised at what your classmates will contribute.

Cloud Tools for Schoolwork

The following cloud tools were popular in 2011 and accessible online for free.

Websites to Create a Presentation

Perhaps the assignment is for a multimedia presentation but Microsoft PowerPoint just isn't cool enough.

Prezi (prezi.com) is a storytelling application that uses a single page with graphics and words placed upon it. You move the view around the page in frames or zoom in and out. Prezi is best for nonlinear presentations where the information can be accessed in any order.

VoiceThread (voicethread.com) is a multimedia slideshow that records conversation using voice or text. You create a presentation using images, videos, and documents and share it with your classmates. They can add comments and doodles for others to see. VoiceThread is best for presentations involving a lot of video and audio.

SlideShare (slideshare.net) is a slide-hosting service used to post Microsoft PowerPoint or Open Office presentations online, and you can limit who has access to them. It also hosts documents, PDFs, and videos, so it's a great website for posting pieces that you need your whole group to use.

Xtranormal (xtranormal.com) is a service that allows you to create an animated video. You choose characters, backgrounds, and give it dialogue. It creates and stores the video.

For a more subtle approach, try Google Search Stories (www.youtube.com/user/SearchStories). By inputting search terms and showing the results in a Google search, you can imply a story. The result is a video showing your searches and highlighting results, all set to music. (You may have seen Google's Super Bowl commercials using this technique.)

To find more presentation tools, search online for *free online presentation software.*

Websites to Create Graphics and Posters

The assignment is for a poster or graphical representation, but you're tired of Microsoft Publisher's clip art.

Glogster (glogster.com) is a social network that allows you to create interactive posters. You insert text, videos, images, audio, and even special effects, and then share the poster.

A Wordle (wordle.net) is a word cloud in an interesting graphical setting. You put in a document, and it counts the number of times that each word appears. It then arranges all the words in a mass, with words used more frequently in a larger font. The result is a jumble of words, with the most important ones popping out. Wordle .net allows you to input your own document and adjust the appearance of the cloud.

SketchUp (sketchup.google.com) is a 3-D modeling program that allows you to design objects and place them in Google Earth. The free version is limited in how much it can do, but it is useful when you want to demonstrate a 3-D concept.

My Fake Wall (myfakewall.com) is a tool that you can use to create fake Facebook pages for a character or historical figure. You could use it to tell about someone's life, including status updates, comments from people the person knew, and photos.

Websites to Record Audio or Make Your Own Music

The assignment needs sound effects . . . legal sound effects.

Audacity (audacity.sourceforge.net) is a free audio editor and recording program. It is fairly easy to use, editing with just copy-and-paste commands.

ccMixter (ccmixter.org) is a music social network that allows users to interact with music in a variety of ways, including creating their own mixes. ccMixter allows the songs created to be used under any Creative Commons license.

The Freesound Project (freesound.org) collects audio samples—not music or songs but actual sounds, such as instruments playing or car horns honking. Because the samples are covered under Creative Commons, you can use them for educational or personal purposes as long as you attribute the owner. Directions on how to do this are on the website.

Websites to Keep Track of Tasks and Responsibilities

The assignment requires a detailed task list, and paper just won't do. There are a few popular cloud-based task-list and note-taking services that allow mobile access. Evernote (evernote.com) is a free note-taking program that you can use online or with a mobile app. You can even do a voice recording. Remember the Milk (rememberthemilk.com) and HiTask (hitask.com) are cloud-based task-list generators.

Sometimes you need to transfer a file between group members, but it's too large to e-mail. There are file storage websites that allow you to save a large file and give others the ability to download it. Try 4shared.com and dropbox.com.

Websites to Keep Track of Other Websites

The assignment has a lot of research, and you need to keep track of and share where you saw what. The answer is a social bookmarking service such as Digg.com or

StumbleUpon.com. Your group can use the same log-in for a single project and see all of the websites linked. You can also put notes for later reference on why the site is useful. A bookmarking service is a great way to compile and combine online research.

Websites for the Aspiring Author

There are social networks just for teens who write. Check these out, and ask your friends what they read.

Inkpop.com: Run by a real publisher, this social network allows teens to post their writings and get feedback from peers and professionals.

TeenInk.com: A safe environment for teen writers and artists.

TeenVoices.com: This website intends to help young activists become proficient journalists as they transform their communities.

gURL.com: This ezine is a place to post writings and drawings as well as find advice on all types of social concerns.

SMITHTeens.com: This publisher collects 6-word memoirs (autobiographical stories in just 6 words) and publishes them. The community to share 6-word memoirs provides much more than just writing support.

LatinitasMagazine.com: This monthly ezine for Latina teens makes it a mission to support teen journalists.

Using Wikipedia for Your Research Paper

If you listen to your teachers, Wikipedia has a very bad reputation! Some teachers even threaten to give a zero on a paper that cites it as a resource! While Wikipedia can have misinformation, it is a really good place to start when you're doing a research paper, especially if you don't know a lot about the topic. It can provide you with search terms to use in finding other resources.

Wikipedia's most powerful tool is the source list at the end of each article. Each fact in Wikipedia is expected to be cited, and links are provided to those other websites. They often include primary and secondary source information from reputable sources such as national newspapers and government information websites. Use Wikipedia to get an overview of your topic, and then follow those sources to get the goodies that you can cite in your paper.

If you want to help your teachers understand why Wikipedia is not an evil research tool, ask them to check Wikipedia's Schools' FAQ for the full story. Get to it from the site's help, then FAQ, then *Schools*.

Notes

1. Vishal Singh, "Immediate Gratification Is the Expectation," *New York Times*, November 20, 2010, www.nytimes.com/interactive/2010/11/21/technology/20101121–brain-interactive.html ?ref=technology.
2. Alycia Birch, "Facebook Instead of Studies Not a Good Thing," *The Record*, March 9, 2010: L-2.

13

HAVE FUN, PLAY GAMES, AVOID BOREDOM

···

"I will play pretty much anything." —Adam, age 17

The Internet is famous for being a fabulous time-wasting tool. You can follow random tangents to all corners of the 'net and even forget what you logged on for in the first place. What do you do when you have nothing to do? Play games!

Games are a fun way to spend time with friends, online and off.

Some Statistics from Pew Internet about Online Game Players

- 50 percent of teens played games "yesterday."
- 86 percent of teens play on a console, such as the Xbox, PlayStation, or Wii.
- 73 percent play games on a desktop or a laptop computer.
- 60 percent use a portable gaming device, such as a Sony PlayStation Portable, a Nintendo DS, or a Game Boy.
- 48 percent use a cell phone or handheld organizer to play games.

Gaming

The most popular way to kill time and boredom online is by playing games. It's so popular that 97 percent of teens play online games, most of them daily. In addition to being fun, online gaming gives teens another place to hang out with friends virtually and be social. Many gaming sites have a social component so that you can share scores, play together, or chat while playing. They also have you register so that you can track your scores, make friends, and decorate your profile. Sounds familiar, doesn't it? Gaming sites are social networks too.

Gamer Netspeak

Netspeak has a place in games as well, especially those that include the ability to chat with other players. Here are some game-specific terms that you may see. Many games have their own language as well.

1337 or 133t or leet = elite, the most skilled players

agg or aggro = when a monster is being aggressive and causing a fight or when the player is aggressive toward a monster alt = alternative character, not your favorite

bfd = big f★★king deal

brb = be right back

clan = a group of players who play together as a club

d/c = disconnected

DL = download

FF = friendly fire

FPS = first-person shooter

ftw = for the win

gg = good game

HP = hit points, your health level

lagger = person whose connection causes the game to lag

lamer = someone who abuses the game by cheating

mmorpg = massively multiplayer online role-playing game, also shortened to
    just *mmo*

noob = newbie—often an insult to somebody who doesn't know much about
    the game

NPC = nonplayer character, the computer's characters

patch = an update to the game

pk = player kill, when fighting other players

POV = point of view

PvP = player versus player

pwnd = owned, defeated, made to look bad

RPG = role-playing game

RTS = real-time strategy game

rush = playing through a level very fast

spawn = place where your character appears after it has been killed

tank = character on a team who can absorb damage

TPS = third-person shooter

twink = a low-level character who has high-level equipment

The Konami Code

The Konami Code is a cheat code that appears in many video games. It was started in 1986 when the gaming company Konami Corporation, which created games such as *Dance Dance Revolution*, put a secret cheat code into its games. Since it has become popular, it has appeared in many different games. Wikipedia maintains a list of places to use the Konomi Code, http://en.wikipedia.org/wiki/List_of_Konami_code_games.

wb = welcome back

XP = experience points

Cheating

Every game has something that gives an advantage to those in the know. Some games plan for them and then carefully leak the information for gamers to find. Other games just have glitches that players can use to their advantage. You can find these by searching online for your game's title and the word *cheat*. Many gamers spend a lot of time finding and discussing cheats.

When you're deciding to use a cheat, consider the moral implications of what you are doing. If you're in a single-player game and only you will ever know about the cheat, it's probably just fine. Finding a way to cheat can help you get past a frustrating part of the game. The word *cheat* has a negative connotation that is not accurate in this circumstance.

However, when it's an online game and others might be harmed by your cheat, it's not a good choice—for example, when a large game such as *World of Warcraft* gets overrun by people who have set computer programs, called *Bots*, to play the game and gather good items and money. Bots change how the game flows and can make it harder and less enjoyable for real players. Be a good person when making choices involving cheating.

Gaming on Your Social Networks

Most social networks include games of some sort. Over 33 percent of teens who play games on Facebook say that they spend at least 50 percent of their time on the site playing games. Many sites, such as Facebook, allow applications that provide games within the framework of the site.

Deciding which games you will play has everything to do with what your friends are playing. Their games will post on their walls updates on their scores and rewards. You can also ask which games they enjoy the most and which they recommend. Find a certain game by searching for the title. Applications require you to give permission to install them—be sure to check your privacy settings to determine what information the game can access through your profile.

Zynga games, such as *Cityville* and *Farmville*, are the most-played games on social networking sites. They stay on top by regularly introducing new and (slightly) different games. The danger in these games is that to have a cool farm or mafia or whatever, you need special game money that is hard to get. You can purchase it with real money, by using a credit card or buying gift cards at gaming stores, and 43 percent of teenage social media users have spent money in this way. Roughly half those teens have an allowance just for online purchases, and 55 percent of those teens feel that it's money well spent. Video gaming industry experts expect US social gaming revenues to surpass $1 billion in 2011! However, ROIWorld's 2010 Teens and Social Networks Study found that 61 percent of teens who have not purchased virtual items for a game believe that it is a waste of money.

Alternatively, you can complete surveys or sign up for free trials to get that special currency. Be wary of these methods! These surveys are meant to get

---

> ## ❗ Reading the Fine Print
>
> ◉ Sometimes the "fine print" on a web page is just that—extremely small. You can zoom in on a web page by using your browser's zoom feature, most often found in the View menu. You can also hold down the control key and roll the scroll button, if your mouse has one.

---

personal information about you to use in marketing campaigns, and they can even sometimes lure you into signing up for services or products you must pay for. Take, for example, the story of Michelle Blitman, age 15, who put her cell phone number into a quiz to get *Farmville* cash. She didn't realize that she was signing up for various pay services until her mother received the $170 phone bill. If you do choose to participate in these surveys, always read the fine print carefully to make sure you that aren't obligating yourself for something you (or your parents) don't want.

Gaming on Game Sites

The Internet is full of sites that host games of all types. There are different types of free gaming options available, from quick, simple games to complex role-playing worlds.

The top minigaming sites at this writing are Y8.com and popcap.com. There are also gaming sections of major sites such as Yahoo or MSN. These sites offer hundreds of quick games that you can play for free without downloading or signing up. They determine which games are most popular on the basis of the number of players and user ratings. They encourage registration so that you can share scores, friend people, add comments, and keep track of your favorite games on your profile.

Some say that these minigames are better and healthier than the more intense games or application games on Facebook. Teen gamers who prefer minigames

Safe and Private in Games

Gamers tend to let their defenses down when they're playing online. You make friends fast and easy when you have a task to complete together and can celebrate successes together. Always remember that the people you meet in games are strangers just as on other social networks. Use the same rules that you use everywhere else—keep your personal information private and protect yourself.

report playing less than 2.5 hours per week, compared to Facebook gamers, who spend more than 6 hours per week on their games. The difference is that minigames aren't built to keep you playing, as the bigger games are.

There are much more in-depth games that can be played online for free. Some of them require that you download the game first, and they all require registration to track your play. Popular games include *Perfect World*, *League of Legends*, *Gaia Online*, *Second Life*, and *Runescape*. In these games, you create a character or avatar and play that person. Some of them are adventure worlds with quests and monsters to beat, while others are more about socializing and building the world. These games often encourage you to subscribe to get more from the game.

Finally, there are games that you purchase and then can play with others online. Blizzard's *World of Warcraft* was the most popular title in this category in 2011. The game itself may cost as much as $100; plus, you probably pay a monthly fee to use the online servers. These games are much more complex and graphically enhanced to give the gamer the best experience possible.

If you would like to play one of these games that requires payment, discuss it with your parents first. It is wise to come to the discussion with an understanding of how much cost is actually associated, and be sure to include any equipment or connection purchases that would be required. If possible, be willing to pay for part of it yourself.

> ### World of Warcraft
>
> The massive multiplayer online game *World of Warcraft* has over 12 million registered players, who spend an average of 80 hours per month in the game. In 6 years, players have spent over 50 billion hours playing, which works out to 5.93 million years. Jane McGonigal, author of the book *Reality Is Broken: Why Games Make Us Better and How They Can Change the World*, pointed out, "We've spent as much time playing *World of Warcraft* as we've spent evolving as a species."[1]

Finding the Good Games

Like everything else on the Internet, finding the good sites is as simple as asking what your friends use. You can also search online to find new sites to try. Find out what your favorite game type is called—puzzle, role-playing, or first-person shooter are common favorites—and search for those terms. Add the words *free online* to find games that you can play without downloading. Check your local library for gaming magazines to find out what games are coming out soon that you may enjoy.

Once you have a favorite game, you may be interested in finding more information about it. Most game sites have a social component in the game or on the website. They may provide forums for discussion about the game, profiles for gamers, and ways to connect with other players. There are often websites to help you do well in the game, both in strategy and in how to cheat. If the website attached to the game you prefer does not include such things, search online for the name of the game and *walkthrough* or *cheat* to find other sites with that information. Be wary of these sites, especially the ones promising cheats, as they often include invasive advertising and even viruses.

> ! **Tell Your Parents! Family Gaming Is Good!**
>
> One study found that teens who play video games with their parents are less likely to become depressed and are generally better behaved. Parents who join in the play may be able to stay more involved and protect their children more efficiently. The creator of the study, Sarah Coyne, of Brigham Young University, says, "When parents are willing to put in the time, they show they're interested."[2]

Defending Gaming

Are video games too violent for kids? This is a question that has gone all the way to the US Supreme Court to determine whether the First Amendment protects the content of games. The case was brought by the Entertainment Merchants Association, a nonprofit organization representing the home entertainment industry. The association was questioning a 2005 California state law that prohibited minors from buying mature-rated games without parental consent.

The video game industry said that laws prohibiting sales of mature games stifle its art form. The ratings system on games is better enforced than movie or music ratings, according to a study done by the Federal Trade Commission. The industry fears that further restrictions would lead to major stores not selling mature-rated games, which would drastically cut profits. "Suddenly games would

> ! **Gaming Consoles**
>
> The major gaming consoles—xBox, Nintendo, and PlayStation—all allow online game play in certain games. The consoles have connections to the Internet and their own social networks where you can friend people, chat via voice or text, and share scores. You have to own the console to take advantage of this network.

What Adults Are Saying

"A good game gives us meaningful accomplishment, clear achievement that we don't necessarily get from real life. In a game, you've beaten level four, the boss monster is dead, you have a badge, and now you have a super laser sword. Real life isn't like that, right?" —Jesse Schell, Carnegie Mellon professor of the practice of entertainment technology[3]

become a regulated commodity, like alcohol and cigarettes," says Ted Price, president of Insomniac Games Inc. "There will be a real chilling effect. We will be more conservative in the ideas that we discuss, we will self-restrict for fear of our games falling under the language in this law."[4]

Proponents of the law restricting violent video game sales, including the law's author, former California state senator Leland Yee, are concerned that the interactive quality of the games desensitizes the player to the violence, which could lead to real-life violence, including school shootings. "Clearly, parents are looking for a valuable tool in raising healthy kids," said Yee, who is a child psychologist. "I am hopeful that the Supreme Court will help empower parents with the ultimate decision over whether or not their children play in a world of violence and murder. The video game industry should not be allowed to put their profit margins over the rights of parents and the well-being of children."[5]

The Supreme Court ruled in June 2011 that video games were protected under the First Amendment. Justice Antonin Scalia wrote, "Like the protected books, plays, and movies that preceded them, video games communicate ideas—and even social messages—through many familiar literary devices (such as characters, dialogue, plot, and music) and through features distinctive to the medium (such as the player's interaction with the virtual world). That suffices to confer First Amendment protection."[6] Because of this ruling, the California state law has been revoked, and the gaming industry has been given some respect for its product. Seth

---

What Teens Are Saying

"When I'm online and bored I visit sites I have marked as favorites, like author's or musician's. I also go to YouTube and watch music videos and other skits I like. I definitely have sites I visit just for fun." —Ariel, age 18

"I like YouTube and various gaming sites because they give me something to do when I'm bored." —Jack C., age 14

"I have an online business so I look to increase my business opportunities and try to find new product to sell. I like to go on education sites and learn. Also, I like to watch documentaries." —Daniel, age 17

Schiesel, journalist for the *New York Times*, said, "The court has ruled that games are art. Now it is up to designers, programmers, artists, writers and executives to show us what art they can produce."[7]

Games are more than just for fun. There is a growing industry of games that teach, train, and give experience in a safe, controlled setting. Military organizations train soldiers; car companies test vehicle safety; surgeons practice tricky surgeries— all in games. Even software giant Microsoft uses games to encourage programmers to complete tedious tasks, such as debugging code. Studies show that gaming can improve hand-eye coordination, decision-making skills, and vision and attention to detail. Games also make a task more interesting, drawing on your natural interest in competition and social ties to other players to keep you engaged.

Studies have shown that gaming has a place in your education as well. The Federation of American Scientists found that students only recall 10 percent of what they read and 20 percent of what they hear, but retention rises to 30 percent if there are visuals too. However, if the students can do the task themselves in a simulation, retention rises to 90 percent.

Schools are finding ways to incorporate games in learning. Quest to Learn, a grade 6–12 school in New York City, supports the digital lives of students in a different sort of learning environment. The students engage in games that require problem solving, and they even code their own games. They must work cooperatively using technology tools to complete complex tasks, such as running an entire city. Grades are based on their competency in the game. The school's website explains, "At Quest we believe that kids learn best when curricular content is presented in an inquiry-based format that contextualizes learning, promotes real world problem solving and creativity. We do this by creating immersive game-like learning environments. At Q2L, students learn by 'taking on' the behaviors and practices of the people in real life knowledge domains. Students learn to be biologists and historians and mathematicians instead of learning about biology or history or math."[8]

Other Fun Stuff

Gaming isn't the only fun thing to do online when you're bored. There are sites featuring funny bumper stickers and signs, meaningful quotations, interesting trivia, or celebrity gossip. You can find websites on just about any topic you can imagine, and you can create your own website about those you couldn't find.

Find these random fun sites the same way that you find everything else—asking friends for advice and searching online. Put random terms into your favorite search engine and see what comes up. And if you're really desperate, search for *fun stuff to do online*. The following are fun sites that were popular in 2011.

Stuff to Do

Cleverbot (http://cleverbot.com): Have a conversation with a computer.

Wikipedia (http://en.wikipedia.org): Search Wikipedia for whatever comes to mind and see where you end up. Alternatively, use the *Random article* link in the left column.

Googlewhack: Using the search engine Google.com, put in 2 words that bring up only 1 search result. Don't use quotation marks to make it a phrase, and use real words. The key is that only a single result appears with that search. Googlewhacks tend to disappear quickly, so be sure to flaunt it if you find one.

Cubescape (www.themaninblue.com/experiment/Cubescape/): Build pictures and cities, one pixel at a time.

ASCII generator (www.network-science.de/ascii/): Put in a word and adjust it to ASCII style.

Mystery Seeker (www.mysteryseeker.com/): Put in a mission, get someone else's answer. Creepy!

Let Me Google That for You (http://lmgtfy.com/): The perfect site for that friend who asks the simplest of questions without looking for themselves. This site allows you to create a search and send the friend the address. When he opens it, it goes to Google, types in the search terms, and shows the results. Snarky but effective.

Stuff to Read

There are people out there writing interesting things that you may enjoy reading and commenting on. Direct your favorite search engine to *blog search engine* to find places to search for blogs on a topic.

Like Cool (www.likecool.com/): A blog of gadgets, design, tech, and more.

MLIA: My Life Is Average (http://mylifeisaverage.com/): Users post tidbits of their day-to-day lives, some funny, some poignant, some uninteresting. Because life is just average.

Cuteoverload.com: More cute animal pictures than you can stand. Seriously.

Stumble Upon (www.stumbleupon.com/): Register and give it some preference information, and this website will give you customized websites on all topics.

What Teens Are Saying

"StumbleUpon!!!!!!!!!!! It's awesome! It just shows me all sorts of random things that it thinks I will like, and it's awesome at finding stuff." —Annie, age 16

Bored.com: Mostly games, but Bored also has quizzes, humor sites, interesting images, and more stuff. Scroll way down to the bottom to find the lists.

Stuff to Look At

Etsy.com: A marketplace for handmade items of all types. There is little you can search for that won't bring up something cool. Start by searching for your favorite movie to see what fans have crafted.

DeviantART (deviantART.com): A place for posting your artwork or browsing other people's amazing (and not so amazing) art.

Webcomics: There are online comics on every topic imaginable. Search for something you enjoy (for instance, soccer, video games, or food) and add the word *webcomic*. There should be navigation buttons on each page that allow you to jump to the first comic if you want to read through what's already happened.

Notes

1. Adam L. Penenbert, "How Video Games Are Infiltrating—and Improving—Every Part of Our Lives," December 13, 2010, www.fastcompany.com/magazine/151/everyones-a-player .html.
2. Elizabeth Lopalto, "Girl Gamers Playing with Parents Are Better Behaved, Study Says," February 1, 2011, www.bloomberg.com/news/2011-02-01/girl-gamers-who-play-with-their-parents-are-better-behaved-study-shows.html.
3. Penenbert, "How Video Games Are Infiltrating."
4. Jess Bravin, "Videogames as Free-Speech Issue," *Wall Street Journal*, November 1, 2010, http://online.wsj.com/article/SB10001424052748704477904575586343221664702.html.

To the Moon!

Google Earth is a 3-D representation of satellite- and street-level photos taken by Google. But did you know that you can use it to see the moon too? Set your favorite search engine to find "google earth" to download the free program. Look under the view menu to find out what is available beyond our planet.

Google Earth isn't just for flying around though. Your teachers may use it to help you learn about geography and history. You can use it to find businesses nearby, link to information and reviews on specific places, and see user photos and videos. You can also explore the ocean floor, track wildlife, or check for traffic jams. It lets you visit shipwrecks and volcanoes. Google Earth shows changes in the world too, as in after a natural disaster or even into history (e.g., back to the 1600s). Additionally, it has ways to see weather patterns, star charts, the moon, and Mars.

Google is constantly adding more content to this amazing program. Check back often to see what's new.

5. Adam J. Keigwin, "Poll: 72 Percent of Adults Support California's Violent Video Game Law," September 14, 2010, http://dist08.casen.govoffice.com/index.asp?Type=B_PR&SEC={EFA496BC-EDC8-4E38-9CC7-68D37AC03DFF}&DE={2F318981-0C0A-4C40-91B7-F68389E3AE18}.

6. Seth Schiesel, "Supreme Court Has Ruled: Now Games Have a Duty," *New York Times*, June 28, 2011, www.nytimes.com/2011/06/29/arts/video-games/what-supreme-court-ruling-on-video-games-means.html.

7. Schiesel, "Supreme Court Has Ruled."

8. Quest to Learn, "FAQs," n.d., http://q2l.org/node/8.

-

KICKING THE HABIT: WHEN AND HOW TO QUIT

"[I would quit] if there was any other way for connecting with people!"
—Priyanka, age 15

Not everyone loves Facebook. In fact, enough users are losing interest that the media has given a name to the phenomenon: Facebook fatigue. ROIWorld's Teens and Social Networks Study found that nearly 20 percent of teens who had Facebook profiles in 2010 have lessened their visits to the page, including not visiting the site at all anymore. Of those, 45 percent say that it's boring, and 27 percent were annoyed by too much activity; furthermore, 28 percent prefer visiting other websites, 16 percent because their friends are using those other sites instead.

Facebook isn't the only online social media site that you can get tired of. In fact, it's a normal step in living an online life. You find a new site, get all excited, and meet new friends and connect with old ones. Then you are comfortable with that site and know how to use it quickly and efficiently. Eventually, you tire of the site, finding less there that entertains you. Maybe your friends move to a new site, or maybe you are the first one to find something better. Eventually, everyone moves from the site to something new, starting the process again.

MySpace is the perfect example of this website lifetime. In 2003 it quickly became the big thing, mostly due to the large marketing company that launched it. MySpace

What Teens Are Saying

"Essentially I only quit social networks when hardly anyone else is using them, they cause me to lose interest or they're just not a good thing to have (like Formspring, re: cyberbullying)." —Grace, age 16

"[I would never quit social networks] because it helps keep you informed on what people you know are up to." —Adam, age 17

"MySpace was probably the most successful of the social networks until everyone left it and joined Facebook, now it's just a ghost town populated only by scene kids. Though the best thing about MySpace is the official band pages that you know are legitimate." —Grace, age 16

had a substantial number of contacts to advertise to. By 2006, MySpace had over 100 million accounts. It overcame Google and YouTube to become the most popular website in the United States in late 2007, with 80 percent of social networking traffic. At the time, Facebook only had 7 percent of the traffic. But that didn't last long; Facebook overtook MySpace on April 19, 2008, moving ahead in rating as determined by Alexa, a company that measures website traffic. Facebook had launched a cleaner, more user-friendly layout that MySpace users, especially teenagers, preferred. MySpace lost users at a rate as high as 10 million accounts in a month! In November 2010, MySpace officially declared Facebook the winner in the social network war, joining the 2 networks so that users could combine information from both.

There are many theories on why MySpace users lost interest and fled to Facebook, but the bottom line is that this is a normal process in the online world. Facebook will have the same problem at some point in the future. In fact, there are hints that it's already in progress. The online world moves at a fast pace, and users—and websites—sometimes struggle to keep up.

Keeping Up with the Fast Pace of the Online World

The trick to not getting overwhelmed with the Internet is to use it in moderation (just like everything else in life). Everyone has a fear of missing out, so much so that it has become a common netspeak term: *FOMO*, fear of missing out. People feel it in different ways, but everyone feels it. It's the fear that you will not be there to witness something amazing or will not realize when something important has happened. Some people obsess over social media sites because they want to be on the front line whenever something happens.

To keep FOMO at bay, make good decisions about whether checking status updates is more important than doing homework or keeping social commitments. Be picky about which sites you use, what you do there, and whose online lives you follow. There are tools discussed in this book that you can use to make your online commitments less time-consuming, such as using a feed reader for blogs.

Information overload is a term used to describe the problems that too much information can cause. Teens deal with information overload a lot better than many adults because they never knew a time when information wasn't constant and everywhere. If you are ever frantic or frustrated because of how much you need to deal with, that's probably information overload. Use the tools that your technology provides to keep the information organized, such as to-do list apps and e-mail filters. Learn when it's right to delete something so you don't have to deal with it anymore. Also, don't hesitate to turn off the thing that is distracting you if you need to focus on something else.

In December 2010, more than 600 students at Shorecrest High School in Seattle did an experiment: they unplugged. For 1 week, they did not use texting, e-mail, or Facebook. They were allowed to make voice calls on their phones, and they used that to keep in touch with family and friends. They found that it was a struggle at first, often responding to incoming messages without remembering that they were not doing that this week. They learned that having a conversation on the phone is a lot harder than it is via text. But after a few days, they reported that it

What Teens Are Saying

"I am really trying to rebel against sites like Facebook, because yeah, sometimes it's an easy way to meet people and stay connected, even to beat boredom, but at what cost? What kind of relationships do you really have through that? Is it worth it?" —Ariel, age 18

"I think most [teens] today love Facebook but also hate it. At school we make jokes about how Facebook is addicting and is dropping your grades. One of them I remember is 'Hi! I'm Mr. Facebook and I made your grades drop.'"
—Priyanka, age 15

"I'm not on any particular social networking site for an extended period of time. If I am, it's because it's running in the background while I do something else."
—Bow, age 20

got easier. One teen said that she started running with her dogs every day; another rekindled a love of basketball; and many of them actually got their homework done! See their videos about the experience at http://shorelinesocialexperiment .blogspot.com/.

Peer Pressure!

All of your friends are on it, and they love it. Should you be there too? Everyone needs to decide what is right for them regardless of what everyone else is doing. Averill says, "I know there are some people who are reluctant to even join sites like this but are being forced to because it is the only way to stay in contact with people anymore, but you don't even need to check the sites themselves, because you can set them up so they e-mail you when you receive something." The cliché

What Teens Are Saying

"It's like a big popularity contest—who can get the most friend requests or get the most pictures tagged." —Abby, age 16, to *CBS News*[1]

"I've wanted to quit social networks. I don't like people asking so many questions, and in a way they are just another way to create more drama. If I quit, I wouldn't have to deal with that. Anyone I needed to reach I could call or text." —Annie, age 16

"I think I will quit social networking after high school or college. If I truly wish to speak to someone, I will call them." —Ava, age 16

"I don't use [social networks] so I even wish other people would quit." —Jack C., age 14

"Teenagers nowadays spend so much time talking to each other on Facebook that when they're actually face-to-face, it's as if they have nothing left to say. They're simply at a loss for words. By becoming a part of the Facebook craze, one is conforming to a trend that is slowly dumbing down a generation and diminishing our social skills." —Joseph, sophomore, in *The Record*[2]

about jumping off a bridge if everyone else is doing it applies here too. The thing is, maybe that bridge is more dangerous for you than for someone else—or your parents believe it is and have given you rules that you want to abide by.

The way to handle peer pressure to join a social network is to stand firm for what you believe in. Make a decision for yourself based on your own beliefs, your parents' input, and your own experience. It's totally fine if it's different than what your friends want, and feel free to tell them so. Take the time to give them your reasons at least once. If they aren't willing to listen, give the reason of "I

Sometimes life moves pretty fast!

prefer not." There is no way to argue that reason away. Ariel has chosen this route, explaining, "Sometimes I want to comment on things, or join them, but I try to resist. I don't want to be consumed by it. I don't like having this feeling that I need to check 50 different things, because that's how I maintain my relationships and stay in the know, it's annoying and I don't want to be ruled by the online world."

When It's More Than You Can Deal With

Depression

One of the biggest issues with social media sites is that they put comparisons of you and your friends right in your face. Some people get upset or depressed when they see that so-and-so has more friends than them or can get a better score in a game. Also, the bit of life that's often portrayed on these sites can make someone else's life seem exciting and much more worthy than your own so-called boring existence. Dwelling on this can make teens feel depressed. Some researchers think this is a social media–caused problem, while others say it's just one more thing that teens have to deal with. Regardless, if you're feeling depressed, consider whether your online life may be making it worse.

> ## What Teens Are Saying
>
> "I think that the social networking sites make it easy to communicate, but to people with an addictive personality or with nothing else to do, it becomes a habit." —Bow, age 20

The most important thing to remember is that it's not real life. Those people who seem to have fabulous lives also have boring and unhappy moments, just as you do. All social media users choose to post news that they think will get them the most attention. It's easy to seem mysterious online, even to people who know you very well.

You can choose whether to visit those sites and how much time you spend on them. Averill suggests, "You can pick and choose what you want to participate in. Not even just choosing what site to log on to, but what you do on that site." Take care of yourself first.

Internet Addiction

Life online can be addicting, especially when real life kind of sucks. Social networks and games are created to keep you interested and wanting more, with each accomplishment giving you a needed tool or opening more levels for you to overcome. Game creators study how to keep a person's attention, and they work very hard to get that perfect balance of challenge without frustration. Meanwhile, real life isn't set up to help you succeed and feel good about it. The success that you feel when you work hard for a goal and meet it in the game can make your hard work in school less meaningful. It's easy to see how a good game can help you to forget homework, friendships, or even food and sleep.

Are You Addicted?

- Do you find yourself staying online longer than you meant to?
- Are you spending more and more time online?
- Have you tried to stop and failed? Do you feel anxious, irritable, or short-tempered when you are trying to cut back?
- Do you constantly think about the website or game when you're doing other things? Do these thoughts distract you from real life?
- Have you lied about how much time you spend online?
- Have you lost a job or a friend because you're too busy online to give them the attention you need?
- Do you feel happy only when you're online?

Addiction comes when you let the online world override the real one. ROIWorld's 2010 Teens and Social Networks Study found that 57 percent of social net gamers find games addicting. Experts such as Dr. Hilarie Cash, who provides therapy for Internet addiction, says that about 10 percent of users allow that addiction to become a problem. If you're putting game life ahead of real life to the extent that you're failing in life, health, or family—you're in trouble.

So, if you're addicted, what do you do? The first thing to do is realize you've got a problem. Think about what you have given up for the website or game, and think about what the site gives you that real life does not. Make lists if that helps you get your thoughts in order. The second thing to do is ask for help. Talk to your parents, trusted adults, school counselor, or doctor about your concerns. Be honest—they can't help you if you don't tell them the full extent of the issue.

What Teens Are Saying

"I actually quit Facebook for a couple months. I deactivated it because I was spending about 18 hours on there each week (while school was on). I also quit because I didn't really have as many social interactions as I would have liked."

—Daniel, age 17

There are things that you can try to deal with the problem without seeking professional help. Start by quitting the website or game for a set period, even just 1 day, and ask your friends and family to help you keep your mind on other topics. If keeping in touch with online friends is a priority, do so via e-mail instead. Quitting the website entirely may seem like the worst thing ever, so put yourself on a schedule that slowly decreases the amount of time that you spend on the site each day or week. If necessary, delete your account. If it's a game, uninstall it from your computer, and give the discs to a friend to hide away.

Be aware that if you found yourself addicted to one website or game, you could easily become addicted to another. Consider finding other hobbies to give you something you love to work for and succeed at. Find ways to get the happiness that the website gave you in real life instead. If you think of real life as a game, each thing that you accomplish would add to your levels and increase your success. Completing the school year with a certain grade point average could be the same as completing a level in the game. Graduating from high school or college could be the equivalent to beating the game's main story line. Think of yourself as the character, and your successes may have more meaning.

If you're finding that you are unable to wean yourself off the website or game or if the online time is getting in the way of your health, it's time to seek professional assistance. Your heath is at risk if you get serious headaches or suffer from deep depression when you're away from the site or if you regularly forget to eat, sleep, or use the bathroom. Talk to your doctor or your counselor at school.

What Teens Are Saying

"I have never used a social networking site. I probably never will. They are just not my style. If you really want to spend all of your time in front of the computer all day, instead of enjoying the beautiful things that God has created for us, then fine. More for the people that care." —Jake, age 13

"As to what to do instead, why not actually physically get together with people and go out and do something. I don't know, read a book, get a hobby, learn a language, volunteer, play a game. I think people should try interacting with the real world a little bit more, and a little less with the virtual." —Ariel, age 18

How to Quit

You may reach a point that being involved with a certain website is no longer right for you. Often this happens naturally, with your visits coming with less frequency without you even noticing. It just doesn't occur to you to go there anymore. This is the easiest way to quit a site because you don't notice it happening.

If it is necessary to quit a site, the best thing to do is to just delete your profile and deactivate your account. Social media sites make this difficult to do because they don't want you to do it (they can count your profile even if you aren't using it anymore). Check the settings tabs for an option to delete your account. If there is no such button, use the help to search for *delete account* or similar keywords. There will likely be a conversation in any forums on the site about how to do this. If even that doesn't lead you to the answer, search the Internet for the name of the site and *delete account*.

Once you have successfully deleted your account, do not attempt to log back in to the site! Sometimes it leaves a door open that will reactivate your account if you try to log in again.

Some sites have the option to deactivate your account instead of completely deleting it. Deactivating will make it look as if you've left the site, but all the content there will be saved. This is a good option if you know you need to walk away from the site for a while but plan on going back someday.

An alternative is to have a friend change your password and not give it to you for a predetermined period. This is especially effective if you just want to quit for finals week. It can also be good if you need to focus on schoolwork on certain days. Have your friend change your password on Sunday night and then reset it Friday afternoon. Be sure to choose a friend whom you can absolutely trust to hold the password for you!

Notes

1. *CBS News*, "'Facebook Depression' Seen as New Risk for Teens," March 28, 2011, www.cbsnews.com/stories/2011/03/28/earlyshow/living/parenting/main20047775.shtml.
2. Joseph V. Cusmano, "Faceless in a Facebook World," *The Record*, May 31, 2009: O-4.

THE INTERNET: THE FINAL FRONTIER?

"In general, the advancement of technology has increased the effectiveness of electronic media tenfold. It's very useful when you need it, and out of the way when you don't." —Bow, age 20

This book focuses on the now of the Internet and social media. In this fast-changing world, things will be different by the time that you read these words. Some things may be drastically changed. So where is it going?

A survey, done in 2010 by the virtual community Habbo Hotel, of 49,000 teens from across the globe, asked just that question. It found that teens believe that information should remain free, most likely in some sort of electronic format. Online safety was of major concern, and most felt that it was their parents' duty to teach them how to be safe and private. They foresee a future where the less formal language and abbreviations used online will permeate spoken language and where virtual worlds will be used to learn and experience the world.

Finding the Next Big Thing

It's time to find a new social network when yours is overrun by your parents and when your friends never log in anymore. This is part of the natural life of a website, and teens are often the first to start leaving a dying site, as well as the first to find the next big thing. But how do you tell what that's going to be? No one really knows. As with everything that goes viral, there is no way of knowing what

What Teens Are Saying

"I think social networking sites will stay as they are. Fun places to talk with friends and play games." —Adam, age 17

"What kind of relationships are we fostering? This question is something I worry about. Maybe someday we'll have a new field of psychology that studies this and we'll have to have new psychiatrists who treat people who are addicted to the online world. Really, what if it becomes a sickness? What if technology does overtake us? By no means am I perfect or completely avoid the online world, neither do I want to, but I do try to limit myself to the most important and spend time away from the Internet as well." —Ariel, age 18

"I think that they will affect teens in the future with spelling, as most teens use text language a lot in their talk. But it is good because it helps us all keep in touch with one another and let us all know what family members and peers are up to." —Daniel, age 17

"I see social networks becoming an increasingly large part of society, as essentially everyone you meet is on at least one of them. It becomes a way of communicating, a way to meet new people, or get to know people better. They also make keeping in contact with people far away so much easier, and organizing events or spreading word about something is convenient and simple." —Grace, age 16

"People are only going to be using social networks to talk to people. They won't get up and go see people, or actually talk to them. We are becoming lazy Americans." —Jake, age 13

"They will kill creativity, dull the mind, and lead to laziness and obesity."
—Ava, age 16

will become popular or when it will happen. Adults who work with and study teens are always looking for the next trend, but even the most promising site can fizzle for no apparent reason.

The spread of a viral hit happens primarily through word of mouth, and there are people in our society who are quietly in positions to make or break a new thing. There are the *innovators*: those friends who seem to always be one of the first in your social circle to post that video or make a profile on a different network. They usually don't even realize they are on the forefront of trends because by the time it really takes off, they've already moved on to the next thing. Then there are the *spotters*—those people who can spot innovators and realize that they are trendsetters. Those people are the ones who draw attention to the new trend. Finally, the rest of the world follows the spotters, often believing the trend came from them in the first place.

The secret is to find the spotters in the people you know (you need not be friends with them to follow their trends) and recognize the trend as it's forming. This is a skill that you can hone by watching the people around you and by paying attention to new trends and who is doing it first. Maybe you will realize you're a spotter or even an innovator!

When it comes to social media, the best thing that you can do is to keep tabs on what your peers—friends and nonfriends—are using. If you hear about a new site and you want more information about it, search the name in your favorite search engine or in Wikipedia. Check out websites such as quantcast.com and alexa.com, analytic websites that measure the use of other sites. They can tell you, for example, up-and-down trends in site traffic, the age of most users, and other demographics.

Social Media Will Affect Your Future School and Career

Remember that everything online stays there forever. So imagine that it's 10 years into the future and your prospective employer is browsing your Facebook profile

Where will you be in twenty years?

What Teens Are Saying

"I see [social networks] becoming a major source of information about people for jobs so they could really see if they want a person. I think that perhaps companies would have company social networks to keep employees informed. In a way, replacing e-mail." —Annie, age 16

"Many employers these days search their job applicants on Facebook to see if they can get a look at what the person is really like. An example of this happened to my friend. One of our mutual friends uploaded pictures of them doing a particular illicit drug, to Facebook, and my friend got extremely upset after seeing them there. If an employer saw that, there is no way they would have hired her." —Grace, age 16

from today. What would that person think of you? While one would hope that future employers and college recruiters would take into account that you were just a teen and have grown and matured considerably in the intervening years, it's still interesting to think about what they might find.

Some day, your social media profile may replace your resume. Rather than you searching for open jobs, companies looking to hire someone may search online profiles to find the perfect match. Hiring managers are already suggesting that job seekers keep their online profiles current and professional.

Colleges are also using social media profiles as part of making decisions about prospective students. Kaplan, a college exam preparation company, found that in 2010, 70 percent of colleges consider students' profiles when determining whether or not to admit them. They're also watching your Twitter and YouTube. An education professional said, "We advise our students to be responsible about what they say and share on social networking sites. People are watching and any profanity or undesired content might affect the school and student's reputation."

Additionally, many colleges are using Facebook to advertise their schools. The same study found that 82 percent of America's top colleges use Facebook in their recruiting process, with 77 percent of them focusing on content for perspective students rather than for current students or alums.

The Internet is becoming an accessible way to build career-oriented networks. The social network LinkedIn focuses on making career connections. Part of your professional career will be finding and keeping professional contacts who can somehow assist your career or your personal growth. It may be a friend who helps you stay on top of what you need to know, a peer who tells you about a job opening in his or her company, or a mentor who strategically assists you in improving yourself. Before the Internet, professionals had to use other means to keep in contact with their network. These days, maintaining a Facebook or LinkedIn friendship may be all that is needed. In a sense, you are building a community of supporters around yourself and, in turn, offering your support to them.

Students are using social media sites to prepare for college and new jobs. Incoming freshmen at a college may form a Facebook group to get to know one another during the summer, creating bonds that will carry over when they meet in real life. Students also use social media profiles to find out information about potential dorm roommates.

In Conclusion

It is clear that today's teens, those who have always had the Internet at their fingertips, will create a new and different world as they become adults. The prospects of such a world are exciting and unimaginable. Congratulations on your future.

Suggested Reading List

Alone Together: Why We Expect More from Technology and Less from Each Other, by Sherry Turkle. New York: Basic Books, 2010.

Creating Content: Maximizing Wikis, Widgets, Blogs, and More, by J. Elizabeth Mills. New York: Rosen Central, 2011.

Cyber-Safe Kids, Cyber-Savvy Teens: Helping Young People Learn to Use the Internet Safely and Responsibly, by Nancy E. Willard. San Francisco: Jossey-Bass, 2007.

The Digital Divide: Arguments for and against Facebook, Google, Texting, and the Age of Social Networking, edited by Mark Bauerlein. New York: Jeremy P. Tarcher, 2011.

The Facebook Effect: The Inside Story of the Company That Is Connecting the World, by David Kirkpatrick. New York: Simon & Schuster, 2010.

Facebook Fairytales: Modern-Day Miracles to Inspire, by Emily Liebert. New York: Skyhorse Publishing, 2010.

Geeks: How Two Lost Boys Rode the Internet out of Idaho, by Jon Katz. New York: Villard Books, 2000.

Grammar Girl's Quick and Dirty Tips for Better Writing, by Mignon Fogarty. New York: Henry Holt and Co., 2008.

Katie.Com: My Story, by Katherine Tarbox. New York: Dutton, 2000.

Online Social Networking, by Carla Mooney. Detroit, MI: Lucent Books/Gale Cengage, 2009.

Online Social Networking, edited by Sylvia Engdahl. Westport, CT: Libraries Unlimited, 2007.

Share This! How You Will Change the World with Social Networking, by Deanna Zandt. San Francisco: Berrett-Koehler Publishers, 2010.

The Social Media Survival Guide: Strategies, Tactics, and Tools for Succeeding in the Social Web, by Deltina Hay. Fresno, CA: Quill Driver Books, 2011.

Social Networking, by Peter K. Ryan. New York: Rosen Central, 2011.

Social Networking, edited by Kenneth Partridge. New York: H. W. Wilson, 2011.

Stealing MySpace: The Battle to Control the Most Popular Website in America, by Julia Angwin. New York: Random House, 2009.

A Teen's Guide to Creating Web Pages and Blogs, by Benjamin Selfridge, Peter Selfridge, and Jennifer Osburn. Waco, TX: Prufrock Press, 2009.

Teens and Privacy, edited by Noel Merino. Detroit, MI: Greenhaven Press, 2011.

Teens, Technology, and Literacy; or, Why Bad Grammar Isn't Always Bad, by Linda W. Braun. Westport, CT: Libraries Unlimited, 2007.

The Twitter Book, by Tim O'Reilly and Sarah Milstein. Sebastopol, CA: O'Reilly, 2009.

Twitterature: The World's Greatest Books in Twenty Tweets or Less, by Alex Aciman and Emmett Rensin. New York: Penguin Books, 2009.

Winter of Our Disconnect: How Three Totally Wired Teenagers (and a Mother Who Slept with Her iPhone) Pulled the Plug on Their Technology and Lived to Tell the Tale, by Susan Maushart. New York: Jeremy P. Tarcher/Penguin, 2010.

Novels

Geek: Fantasy Novel, by E. Archer. New York: Scholastic Press, 2011.

Geektastic: Stories from the Nerd Herd, edited by Holly Black and Cecil Castellucci. New York: Little, Brown & Co., 2009.

Little Brother, by Cory Doctorow. New York: Tor, 2008.

Perfect Cover, by Jennifer Lynn Barnes. New York: Laurel-Leaf Books, 2008.

Train_man, Densha Otoko, by Hidenori Hara. San Francisco, CA: VIZ Media, 2006.

TTFN, by Lauren Myracle. New York: Amulet Books, 2006.

Unfriended: A Top 8 Novel, by Katie Finn. New York: Point, 2011.

Index

4chan.org, 69, 72–73

4shared.com, 210

Abby, 233

Adam, 12, 24, 32, 83, 88, 97, 105, 115, 117, 127, 148, 169, 181, 193, 203, 205, 213, 230, 242

addiction, 235–37

advertisements, 139, 140–41, 142–44, 149, 175, 190, 200

Ahmed, Shawn, 139–41

Alcorn, Angela, 37

Allen, Lily, 168

AltaVista (search engine), 188

Alycia, 202

AMillionThanks.org, 142

Android, 123. *See also* mobile devices

Annie, 14, 17, 24, 28, 34, 60, 82, 86, 97, 111, 115, 123, 126, 128, 143, 148, 226, 233, 245

AOL Instant Messenger, 112

applications. *See* apps

apps, 87–93, 157, 206, 218, 231; mobile, 127–28

Ariane, 73

Ariel, 10, 12, 58, 150, 171, 179, 186, 191, 197, 199, 223, 232, 234, 238, 242

ASCII generator, 225

Audacity, 210

audio recorders, 210

Ausland, Mimi, 138

authorship, 211

Ava, 10, 14, 24, 28, 32, 55, 57, 65, 97, 106, 117, 123, 127, 193, 233, 242

Averill, 12, 17, 23, 28, 32, 73, 97, 111, 114, 117, 123, 126, 148, 173, 175, 181, 188, 202, 203, 232, 235

Baron, Naomi, 14

Bazelon, Emily, 61–62

bebo.com, 77–78

Bieber, Justin, 66, 75, 80, 154, 196, 198

Billboard.com, 174

Bischof, Chelsea, 62

Blackberry. *See* mobile devices

Blackboard (online collaboration

tool), 205

The Blair Witch Project, 161

Blip.fm, 173

Blitman, Michelle, 218

blog readers, 109

Blogger.com, 108

blogs, 8, 15, 105–10, 198, 225

Blount, Bryant, 195

bookmarking, 211–12

Bored.com, 226

bots, 217

Bow, 7, 12, 18, 25, 33, 34, 41, 70, 115, 123, 126, 181, 205, 232, 235, 241

boyd, danah, 57, 90

Bregy, Michael, 132

Bubble Ball (puzzle game app), 129

Buck, James, 88–89

Bullock, Chad, 139

bullying. *See* cyberbulling

Burstein, David, 141

career, 243–45

Carlos, 14

Caroline, 45

Cash, Hilarie, 236

ccMixter, 210

celebrities, 191–200

cellphone. *See* mobile devices

Chance, Greyson, 159–60

Chang, Alison, 190

Chapman, Peter, 29

Charity Navigator, 138–39

ChatRoulette, 69, 71

chatting, 8, 13, 71, 91, 99, 111–14, 120, 204, 221; voice, 114, 221

Children's Online Privacy Protection Act of 1998, 27, 37–38

Cleverbot, 224

clip art, 209

cloud, 202–3, 208

Coleman, Monique, 135

college, 32, 80, 117, 128, 137, 237, 245–46

commenting, 7, 15, 60, 72, 87, 148, 149, 150–52, 154, 163, 173, 174–75, 177, 179, 180, 192, 200, 203, 208, 209, 218, 225, 234

communication, 9, 10, 13–16, 35, 86, 93–98, 108, 121–22, 135, 207, 242

community service. *See* volunteerism

computer security, 35

computer virus, 26, 170–72

consumerism, 142–44

Cook, Catherine, 101

Cook, David, 101

Cook, Geoff, 11

copyright, 49–52, 131, 161, 162, 163, 164, 168–70, 180, 188–89, 190

Coyne, Sarah, 221

Craigslist.com, 20

Creative Commons, 50–52, 189–90, 210

Cruikshank, Lucas, 198

Cubescape, 225

culture change, 9–10, 20, 93, 201, 243

CuteOverload.com, 225

cyberbullying, 12, 24, 55–75, 132, 140, 151, 230; cause of, 60–62; documenting, 67; effect of, 59–60; friends, 68–69; on YouTube, 150–51; what to do, 63–69

Cyrus, Miley, 197–8

Daniel, 13, 24, 28, 32, 34, 41, 57, 86, 105, 106, 111, 115, 117, 140, 143, 151, 159, 185, 186, 193, 203, 223, 237, 242

dashboard, 92

dating, 63, 91–92

Davies-Carr, Howard, 164

deactivating your account, 239

DeGeneres, Ellen, 75, 159

deleting your account, 238

depression, 234–35

deviantART.com, 187, 226

DeWolfe, Chris, 168

Digg, 79, 200, 210

DiNucci, Darcy, 8

Doctorow, Cory, 96

Domenech, Daniel A., 132

DoSomething.org, 138, 139

driving, 124–27

droid. *See* android

dropbox.com, 210

Duncan, Arne, 62

e-book readers, 120, 128–29, 206

education. *See* school

e-mail, 116–17, 120, 204, 205, 210

emoticons, 93, 96–98

Entertainment Merchants Association, 221–22

Etsy.com, 226

Evernote (note-taking program), 210

Facebook, 8, 9, 11, 12, 18, 19, 28, 32, 77, 80, 86, 90, 136, 147, 167, 232, 237, 245, 246; advertising on, 200; bullying, 58, 69, 72, 73; celebrities on, 193, 196; chatting on, 111; e-mail/messaging, 115–17; fatigue, 30, 229–33, 237; for school, 203–5; games on, 217–19; getting started, 78–85; history of, 100, 170; mobile, 121; music on, 172–73; photos on, 177–85; profiles, 83–85, 243; romance, 41, 45; safety and privacy, 18, 19, 24, 27, 28, 29, 30, 33; stalking, 42; statistics, 9, 110, 116, 121, 219, 229, 230; username, 18, 79–81

Fake, Caterina, 184

FameCount.com, 196

fanfic, 12

Fanning, Shawn, 170

fear of missing out, 231

Federman, Charlie, 144

feed readers, 109

FeedDemon.com, 109

file transfer, 210

Fleming, Shauna Lynn, 142

Flickr.com, 8, 179, 181, 182, 183, 184, 185, 189–90

FlickrCC, 188

Formspring, 69, 70, 72, 230

FourSquare, 143

The Fray, 175

Fred Figglehorn. *See* Cruikshank, Lucas

free speech, 62–63, 221–23

The Freesound Project, 210

friend requests. *See* friending

friending, 7, 18–19, 25, 28, 30, 32, 35, 58, 64, 81–83, 91, 113, 130, 143, 180, 204, 218, 221, 233, 243

friendships, 18–19, 43, 105, 117, 203, 232, 242

Friendster, 19, 78

FTP. *See* file transfer

fun stuff, 224–26

future, 16, 19, 244–46

Gaia Online (game), 219

games, 8, 33, 57, 89–90, 120, 128, 129, 214–24, 235–37, 242; cheating, 216–17, 220; defending, 221–24

geotagging, 180

getting started, 78–79

Glieberman, Owen, 199

Glogster.com, 209

Google AdSense, 200

Google Apps for Education, 205

Google Docs, 205, 207

Google Earth, 209, 227

Google Reader, 109

Google Search Stories, 209

Google, 78, 80, 92, 147, 151, 225, 230; image search, 188; yourself, 37–38

Google+, 77

Googlewhack, 225

Gossett, Michael, 197–98

Grace, 13, 17, 18, 29, 45, 72, 82, 86, 88, 110, 111, 117, 122, 126, 140, 150, 159, 165, 170, 171, 230, 242, 245

graphics, 209

Green, Hank, 105, 140

Green, John, 105, 140

Grooveshark.com, 173, 174

gURL.com, 211

Habbo Hotel, 241

Hall, Ashleigh, 29

Healy, Melissa, 10

Hessert, Kathleen, 195

Hi5.com, 77

Hill, Mark, 161

HiTask (task-list generator), 210

Hocking, Amanda, 130

Honesty Box, 69, 70, 73

Hughes, Chris, 141

Hulu.com, 147, 148

Hurley, Chad, 74

Hype Machine, 174

icanhascheezeburger.com, 185–87

ICQ, 112

IM. *See* instant messaging

ImageShack.us, 180

IMDB.com, 193

iMovie, 156

influencers, 11

information overload, 231

Inkpop.com, 211

innovators, 243

instant messaging (IM), 14, 63, 99, 111–14, 204

Internet contract, 36–37

iPad. *See* mobile devices

iPhone, 120, 123. *See also* mobile devices

It Gets Better Project, 140

Ito, Mizuko, 15

iTunes, 130, 167, 169, 171, 174

Jack C., 13, 25, 32, 33, 34, 41, 57, 58, 70, 105, 106, 115, 123, 127, 129, 131, 147, 165, 171, 193, 223, 233

Jack S., 32, 79, 86, 106, 111, 117, 123, 126, 179

Jade, 38–39, 55, 58, 60, 65, 77, 83, 106, 192, 198

Jake, 25, 27, 34, 41, 65, 82, 143, 148, 151, 186, 192, 238, 242

Joseph, 233

Jumo.com, 138

Karim, Jawed, 150

Kazaa, 169

Kindle. *See* e-book readers

Kingston, Sean, 167–68

Konami Code, 216

Kurzweil, Ray, 119

language, 16

Last.fm, 174

LatinitasMagazine.com, 211

leadership, 136

League of Legends (game), 219

leet speak, 96

Let Me Google That for You, 225

library, 128, 171, 203, 204

LikeCool.com, 225

liking, 151

LinkedIn, 78, 246

literacy, 15, 16

LiveJournal.com, 108

lolcats, 185–87

lolspeak, 186

Loorz, Alec, 137

Ludwig, Miles, 163–64

Lur, Xavier, 183

Madden, Mary, 17

Magid, Larry, 18

Maislos, Ariel, 17

manners. *See* netiquette

Maree, Mohammed, 88–89

McBrine, Craig, 156–57

McGonigal, Jane, 220

Meebo.com, 113

meme, 73

Mezrich, Ben, 100

Michaelson, Ingrid, 168, 175

microblogging. *See* status updates

Microsoft, 223

Microsoft Live@edu, 205

Microsoft Movie Maker, 156

Microsoft Word, 189

military, 223

MLIA: My Life Is Average, 225

mobile devices, 119–33, 155; at school, 203, 206

Moodle (online collaboration tool), 202, 205

"mouse trapping," 52

Ms. Twixt, 132

MSN, 218

MTV, 167, 174–75

MTV's Act, 138

multitasking, 15, 35

music, 120, 130, 147, 150–51, 164, 165–76, 210; at school, 203

Mustafa, Isaiah, 143–44

MyFakeWall.com, 209

MySpace.com, 16, 21, 77, 82, 84–85, 86, 101, 141, 229–30; music, 165, 167–68, 173, 174

Mystery Seeker, 225

Myxer.com, 129

MyYearbook.com, 11, 77, 101

Napster, 170

Nay, Robert, 129

Nerdfighters, 105, 140

Netflix, 148

netiquette, 93, 98–99

netspeak, 13–14, 93–96, 125, 186, 231; in gaming, 214–16; on Twitter, 89

Nicole, 14

Niki, 13, 17, 25, 28, 33, 34, 41, 82, 83, 86, 90, 97, 106, 111, 116, 123, 126,

148, 169, 171, 173, 177, 185, 203, 207

Ning.com, 78, 103, 104–5, 205

Nook. *See* e-book readers

O'Brien, Sally, 135

O'Neal, Shaquille, 195

Obama, Barack, 141–42, 194, 196

Orkut.com, 78

Ortiz, Steven, 20

Paint.NET, 181

"page jacking," 52

Pandora.com, 173, 174

parents, 9, 11, 18, 20, 29, 30–37, 44,
    55, 64, 70, 79, 90, 121–22, 130,
    172, 218, 219, 221, 233, 236, 241

Parker, Sean, 170

passwords, 38–40, 58, 239

Paulsen, Ken, 62

peer pressure, 232–34

Peguine, Dan, 70

Perfect World (game), 219

personal journals. *See* blogs

phone. *See* mobile devices

PhoneZoo.com, 129, 131

Photobucket.com, 180, 182, 184–85,
    187–88

photos, 177–90; editing, 182–85;
    profile, 84

Photoscape.org, 181

Photoshop, 184

Picasa, 179, 181

Picnik, 181, 185

Ping, 167

pixlr.com, 185

PlumWillow (shopping site), 144

Podium, 202

political activism, 141–42

popcap.com, 218

presentation software, 208–9

Prezi.com, 207, 208

Price, Ted, 221–22

Prince, Phoebe, 61–62

privacy, 16–18, 26, 36, 37–38, 79, 88,
    93, 108, 112, 130, 142–43, 155,
    191, 219; of celebrities, 194, 196;
    on Facebook, 27, 30

Priyanka, 11, 28, 33, 60, 65, 86, 97,
    114, 115, 119, 126, 181, 193, 201,
    229, 232

profile, 83–84, 91–92, 101, 179

Project for Awesome, 105, 140

Project Vote Smart, 142

QR codes, 121

Qualls, Ashley, 100–101

Quest to Learn, 224

quitting (delete account), 238–39

quizzes, 90–91, 226

reading comprehension, 11, 15

relationships. *See* dating; romance

Remember the Milk (task-list generator), 210

resume, 245

ringtones, 129–31

RockTheVote.org, 142

romance, 40–45. *See also* dating

Rotem, J. R., 167–68

RSS (really simple syndication), 109

Runescape (game), 219

Sacchetti, Sarahjane, 70

safety, 11, 23–53, 57, 79, 112, 130, 155, 219, 241; from bullies, 64; rules, 23–26

Sandberg, Sheryl, 116

Savage, Dan, 140

Scalia, Antonin, 222

Schell, Jesse, 222

Schiesel, Seth, 222–23

school, 15, 66, 123, 128, 131–32, 201–6, 224

school skills, 15, 223; group work, 205, 206–8

searching tips, 104, 153, 154–55, 188, 198

Second Life (game), 219

sexting, 122–24

sharing, 7, 9, 87, 148, 149, 151, 163,

199–200, 209, 218

SketchUp, 209

Skype.com, 71, 114

SlideShare, 208

smartphone. *See* mobile devices

Smith, Jaden, 198–99

SMITHTeens.com, 211

snopes.com, 99

social media, 7–8, 77–80, 103; affecting communication, 9; definition of, 8; finding sites, 79, 108, 113–14, 128, 137–28, 152–54, 172–75, 177, 187–88, 191–95, 197, 220, 224, 243; keeping up with, 92, 231–32

social networking. *See* social media

social skills, 10–12, 16

social steganography, 90

status updates, 85–87, 106, 107

Stewart, Morgan, 116

Streetside Stories, 141

StumbleUpon.com, 79, 211, 225, 226

Summers, Amy, 42

Sweeney, Sarah M., 16

tablets, 119

Tagged.com, 77

tagging, 162, 179, 180, 181

Tagliamonte, Sali, 15

task lists, 210

teachingparentstech.com, 30

technology skills, 16, 19–20

Technorati, 109

TeenInk.com, 211

TeenVoices.com, 211

Tele2, 161–62

telephone. *See* mobile devices

television, 128

Ternovskiy, Andrey, 71

texting, 15, 108, 117, 120–27, 135, 231–32; for school, 205, 206; sexting, 122–24; while driving, 125–27

ThatsNotCool.com, 63

Thomas, 103

Thomas-Rasset, Jammie, 169

Timberlake, Justin, 167

time management, 86, 210

trivia, 90–91, 138, 174, 175, 224

Tumblr.com, 110

Tuttle, Kate, 124

Twitter.com, 8, 12, 78, 79, 80, 86, 88–89, 107, 135, 136, 179, 195, 196, 245; abbreviations, 89

Uncultured Project, 140

username, 80–81

Vevo.com, 165–67, 173

Vicki, 86

videos, 147–64

Vimeo.com, 147

viral content, 23, 143, 152, 153, 159–64, 198, 199–200, 241–43

Virgin Mobile Pty Ltd, 190

Vishal, 202

vlogging, 105, 159, 163

VoiceThread, 208

Volodkin, Anthony, 174

volunteerism, 135–41

Web 2.0, 8

webcomics, 226

website evaluation, 45–50

whateverlife.com, 100–101

Wikia.com, 103

wikimedia.com, 188

Wikipedia.org, 103–5, 109, 175, 195, 197, 216, 224, 243; for school, 211–12

wikis, 103–4, 205

Windows Live, 112

Wordle.com, 209

WordPress.com, 108

World of Warcraft (game), 216–17, 219, 220

writing skills, 13–15, 108, 242

Xanga, 106

Xtranormal, 209

Y8.com, 218

Yahoo, 188, 218

Yahoo Instant Messager, 112

Yee, Leland, 222

YouthNoise.com, 138

YouTube.com, 8, 74, 75, 93, 139–41, 147, 148, 149–52, 153–54, 157, 159, 160, 162–63, 165, 167, 171, 173, 194, 196, 198, 223, 230, 245

Zuckerberg, Mark, 100

Zynga games, 217

About the Author

Jenna Obee is the teen services librarian for the Standley Lake Public Library of the Jefferson County Public Library system (Colorado). She has served as the chair of the Teen Advocates Round Table, a committee of teen services librarians, and is part of a Teen Advisory Board for librarians. Obee is currently a part of the Colorado Teen Literature Conference planning committee and the Colorado Blue Spruce Book Award planning committee. She has contributed to books, articles, and bibliographies, including *More Than MySpace* (2009) and *The Continuum Encyclopedia of Young Adult Literature* (2005).

CPSIA information can be obtained at www.ICGtesting.com
Printed in the USA
BVOW061102191012

303278BV00003B/2/P